Teachin' It!

Teachin' It!

Breakout Moves That Break Down Barriers for Community College Students

FELICIA DARLING

TEACHERS COLLEGE PRESS

TEACHERS COLLEGE | COLUMBIA UNIVERSITY

NEW YORK AND LONDON

Published by Teachers College Press, 1234 Amsterdam Avenue, New York, NY 10027

Cover design by adam b. bohannon. Cover photo by michaeljung / Shutterstock.

Library of Congress Cataloging-in-Publication Data is available at loc.gov

ISBN 978-0-8077-6158-8 (paper)
ISBN 978-0-8077-6184-7 (hardcover)
ISBN 978-0-8077-7799-2 (ebook)

Printed on acid-free paper
Manufactured in the United States of America

Contents

Preface

By the age of 19, I had already faced homelessness; survived sexual assaults by knife and gun; and overcome other challenges common for our students who have lived in poverty. Although neither of my parents, nor any of my five siblings, had obtained a bachelor's degree, I knew that a college education was crucial for my financial success. When I was 20, I hitchhiked the 360 miles to the University of Vermont (UVM) to "go to college." I wandered in and around the forest of colossal buildings on the UVM campus. Ultimately, I hitchhiked home without any better idea about how to gain admission to a university. That was my first college experience. My second was enrolling at Community College of Vermont at age 23.

As a first-generation college student, I made a long journey from my first community college course to attaining my PhD at age 54. For almost 30 years, I supported the success of students historically underrepresented among those with 4-year degrees. I taught math and education courses in urban high schools, in probation and parole programs, community colleges, and universities. In 2016, I attained a PhD in Math Education from Stanford University, where I was immersed in the equity education research of scholars like Jo Boaler, Carol Dweck, Claude Goldenberg, Rachel Lotan, Kenji Hakuta, and Claude Steele. Also at Stanford I conducted my own research around redressing inequity in Yucatec Maya math classrooms in the Yucatán. Today, I weave ideas gleaned from these experiences into my classroom practice as I teach math in the College Skills Department at Santa Rosa Junior College.

Acknowledgments

Thanks to: Avery Occaso for illustrating, editing, proofing; Alia Thabit for providing marketing, technological, and moral support; Dr. Jo Boaler for breathing life into my own big dreams at Stanford; Dr. Claude Goldenberg for not giving up on me at Stanford and giving me feedback on the manuscript; Mark Felton and faculty in the Secondary Education Department at San José State University for teaching me how to teach educational psychology; Santa Rosa Junior College experts President Dr. Frank Chong, Vice President Dr. Mary Kay Rudolph, Ann Foster, Dr. KC Greaney, Dr. Robert Holcomb, Jerry Miller, Regina Guerra, Dan Munton, Jessica Munton, Laura Aspinall, Geoff Navarro, Byron Reaves, Audrey Schell, Carlos Valencia, Rafael Vasquez, Juan Soto, Amy Rosciele Flores, Pattie Myers, Emily Hansen, and Abigail Zoger; Stanford Hume Writing Center's Dr. Emily Polk, Dr. Kris Kamrath, and Dr. Maxe Crandall for teaching me to write; and Amanda Takemoto, Dr. Daisy McCoy, Cherry Hebert, Stewart Hoyt, Dr. Linda Metzke, and Ann Traverso for helping me when I was overcoming poverty in Vermont.

Introduction

I wrote *Teachin' It!* to help instructors help students like me, first-generation college students navigating the unfamiliar terrain of college. Also, I wrote *Teachin' It!* to bolster the success of students of color, LGBTQ+ students, students with disabilities, and other students who are driven to get a college education, but who may feel like cultural outsiders on community college campuses. I wrote *Teachin' It!* to help instructors design asset-based instruction—to help instructors create inclusive, engaging, interactive learning environments where students from all backgrounds are motivated to experiment, take risks, make mistakes, share their unique perspectives, evolve as powerful lifelong learners, and feel the deep satisfaction of, as one community college student put it, breathing life into students' dreams. That *is* asset-based instruction. It is the "It," with a capital I, in *Teachin' It!*

Teachin' It! offers research-based, classroom-level solutions that improve retention, completion, and transfer rates of students in community colleges and other open-access colleges. The Teachin' It! model delivers strategies that redress the wide range of gaps in knowledge and skills in community college classrooms while simultaneously holding all students to the same high standards. These strategies disrupt systemic inequity at the classroom level, too, thus equalizing the playing field for students who historically have been underrepresented among those with 4-year degrees.

Similar to findings from my research in Yucatec Maya classrooms, community college students come to our classes with cultural assets that often are overwritten instead of valued. To address this, *Teachin' It!* describes how to deliver asset-based instruction that illuminates students' unique approaches in order to optimize learning potential. This asset-based approach involves creating inclusive, dynamic instruction that builds upon the unique contributions of students from all backgrounds and invites all students to engage in inquiry-based learning in groups.

Teachin It! offers new approaches described by seasoned community college instructors. It presents a fresh look at enduring educational psychology theory and translates cutting-edge cognition and neuroscience research using real-life classroom examples. Furthermore, by weaving in student narratives, instructor stories, illustrations, and cartoons, it explains how the research is connected to instruction. Individual instructors will walk away with 50 new strategies they can pilot in their own disciplines and classrooms the very next day.

Although this book is geared specifically toward community college and open-access college instructors, many of the principles discussed are relevant to the K–12 or university settings.

The strategies, perspectives, and mindset in the chapters that follow are not age-limited or discipline-specific, and thread learning, life, self-management, and social–emotional skills and well-being into academic learning. Readers will find the following in the book's 10 chapters:

Chapter 1 discusses what makes community college instructors powerful, and describes the process through which instructors refine their instruction to bolster the success of community college students.

Chapter 2 describes stories of community college students' challenges and assets, and some challenges unique to community colleges and open-access colleges.

Chapter 3 discusses how an instructor can cultivate an equity mindset and presents ideas for how to nurture positive academic mindsets in students. It offers ways to reach and mentor students who are from different ethnic/racial or class backgrounds than one's own.

Chapter 4 illustrates key educational psychology theory that is essential for facilitating inquiry-based group instruction.

Chapter 5 offers principles and high-impact strategies to facilitate inquiry-based group learning. It explains how to launch an inquiry-based interactive learning class and how to build a strong community of learners to support this model of instruction.

Chapter 6 discusses important equity research and how to bolster the success of African American males in higher education.

Chapter 7 discusses necessary college skills and how to support the success of Latinx students seeking 4-year degrees.

Chapter 8 describes funds of knowledge of bilingual students and provides specific strategies to support their success.

Chapter 9 frames the teaching of college and career skills as equity moves, and describes specific strategies to teach these skills while honoring students' identities.

Chapter 10 stresses the importance of teaching life skills, incorporating key principles of this book into online courses, and collaborating with colleagues.

A Note About Activities. Throughout the book, when an activity is marked in bold, you can learn more about it by visiting the resources page of www.feliciadarling.com.

A Note About Terminology. Throughout the book, the terms *ethnic/racial* or *ethnicity/race* describe the concept that historically has been referred to as *race*. Also, the term *African American* is used, generally. However, the term *Black* is used to reference research that uses this term. Finally, both "Black" and "White" will be capitalized no matter the usage.

Throughout this book the term *Latinx* is used to describe students from Latin American or Spanish-speaking backgrounds. *Latino* and *Latina* are gender-specific terms and do not include students who identify as non-cisgender, a person's sense of identity when it is not the same as their birth sex. Sometimes the term *Hispanic* is used—especially when authors are referring to a specific study that uses this term.

—*Dr. Felicia Darling, Santa Rosa, CA*

CHAPTER 1

Educators Are Experts, Improvisational Artists, Researchers

> An expert is [someone] who has made all of the mistakes one can make in a narrow field.
>
> —Niels Bohr

If you have experimented with instructional approaches, learned from your mistakes, and refined your instruction for years, then you are an expert. If you are just beginning your career as a community college instructor, then you are a budding expert. Whichever you are, this book offers ideas to help community college students become powerful learners, and this chapter begins with a discussion of what makes powerful instructors.

INSTRUCTORS ARE EXPERTS AND IMPROVISATIONAL ARTISTS

Instructors are expert weavers. We weave together strands from our own personal experiences, cultural backgrounds, content knowledge, instructional knowledge, and education into the complex tapestry that is our unique classroom instruction. In addition, we weave into instruction the fibers of our beliefs, attitudes, values, expectations, and mindsets about students, learning, and society. This constellation of beliefs, attitudes, content knowledge, and instructional expertise constitutes an instructor's schema. According to developmental psychologist Jean Piaget (1952), a schema is "a cohesive, repeatable action sequence possessing component actions that are tightly interconnected and governed by a core meaning" (p. 7). Basically, a schema is the matrix of interconnected bits of knowledge stored in our brains. It is organized according to our core value systems. Research indicates that experienced educators have well-elaborated, complex schemas (Borko & Whitcomb, 2008), and all instructors draw from these schemas to make rapid-fire decisions every day while teaching a class. Also, we draw from these schemas to design, deliver, and refine curriculum and instruction each week, month, and year. Because an instructor's schema is idiosyncratic and as unique as a signature or fingerprint, this process is specific to each instructor.

Educators' schemas change over time. When educators begin teaching, they may draw disproportionally from their own past experiences as students to inform their instruction—and rely predominantly on direct instruction. As educators gain new knowledge, they refine their schemas and their instructional techniques. Interviews that I conducted with community college instructors confirmed that instructors' views of education evolve and correspondingly transform how they teach. Carlos Valencia, a math instructor in the College Skills Department at Santa Rosa Junior College (SRJC), shifted his approach away from primarily lecturing content to a more social and conceptual approach. When he first started teaching, he thought that "students were empty vessels that I filled with knowledge" and that he would just focus on "communicating the content really well and students will walk away knowing what they need to know." As he became informed by experience, educational psychology, and education coursework, Carlos made the shift away from focusing on "teaching content knowledge" toward focusing on "a relational approach," building connections with students. Also, he made the shift from focusing on procedural, algorithmic knowledge toward an approach that deepened conceptual understanding. For example, instead of just *showing* students the algorithm or rule for multiplying fractions, he asks students, "Why do we multiply the numerators and denominators *across* when we multiply?" Then, students discuss their answers in groups to deepen their conceptual understanding and to stimulate their prior knowledge around the concept. *Teachin' It!* offers a buffet of research, strategies, and practical ideas for instructors to integrate into their existing schemas to refine their instruction and bolster the success of even more students.

Professional Development Worthy of Instructor Experts

Merriam Webster defines pedagogy as "the art, science, or profession of teaching." However, the word *pedagogue* has acquired some negative connotations. In Greek, a *paidagogos* was a slave who led boys to school

Figure 1.1. A Deprofessionalizing Model of PD

and back, and also taught them manners and tutored them after school. In time, pedagogue came to mean simply "teacher." Today the word often means a stuffy, boring teacher, so the term *instructional practices* is used instead of "pedagogy" in this book.

Teachin' It! not only describes an asset-based model of instruction that illuminates all students' assets in order to actualize their full learning potential, but also promotes an asset-based approach to professional development (PD) for educators. This approach regards instructors as innovative experts. The outdated term *training* implied a deprofessionalizing model of professional development. Instead, *Teachin' It!* talks about moves: instructor, equity, empathy, facilitator, mentor, and coaching moves, because "moves" are a form of unique self-expression. Educators are not robots to be trained in technical skills (Figure 1.1).

In the asset-based model of professional development, educators are regarded as experts in their fields and powerful improvisational artists (see Figure 1.2). In asset-based PD, instructors' unique expertise is leveraged to help them optimize their instructional potential. In an asset-based model, instructors are offered a buffet of research and strategy options, and exercise their agency to select what is relevant to their discipline and students and compatible with their teaching styles. They decide how to

Figure 1.2. An Asset-Based Model of PD

adapt their schemas to accommodate these new ideas. Then, they use their autonomy and improvisational skills to express how they are going to teach their content, facilitate productive discussions, mentor students, support student success, or create a safe learning environment for all students.

INSTRUCTORS ARE RESEARCHERS

Instructors are expert researchers who experiment and study how to improve instruction to bolster student learning. They are continuously engaged in a cycle of instruction improvement. When an instructor pilots a new strategy, refines it, and tries it again, they engage in the process of instruction improvement.

The Cycle of Instruction Improvement

In Phase 1 of this cycle of instruction improvement, educators pilot a strategy, instructional approach, or activity (see Figure 1.3). In Phase 2,

Figure 1.3. Continuous Cycle of Instruction Improvement

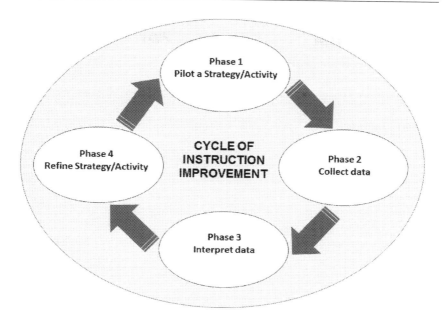

instructors elicit and collect evidence or data on how well this strategy is working. In Phase 3, instructors interpret these data. Did this strategy work or not? Why didn't it work? What could I do to continue to revise this strategy or activity to maximize student learning? In Phase 4, instructors pilot this newly refined strategy. All instructors seeking to improve their instruction engage in an iterative improvement process on a minute-by-minute, class session, unit, or semester basis.

As one example, Lauralyn Larsen, an instructor in Work Experience, ends an activity by asking students, "What is the muddiest point? What is the clearest point?" This is a great way to solicit evidence (Phase 2) about how well an activity went for students and to start thinking about how to refine instruction. The following example illustrates the complete cycle of instruction improvement. A U.S. history instructor pilots an activity (Phase 1) where a group of four students read four different parts of a historical artifact during class and then explain their section to the rest of the group. At the end of the activity, the instructor collects evidence of learning (Phase 2) by asking students, "What is the muddiest/clearest point?" In Phase 3, he interprets their responses as indicating that they are struggling with a significant part of the content. He decides that he will refine this activity so that next time students will read their parts of the artifact *before* class and write answers to a set of guiding questions *before* sharing out in groups during class (Phase 4).

What Counts as Evidence or Data?

Evidence, or data in the case of the cycle of continuous improvement of instruction, is anything that instructors can observe and interpret that indicates that the instructional strategy did or did not have the desired effect on student learning. As attributed to the thought leader Peter Drucker, "If it can be measured, then it can be improved." Most things can be measured, if you have the right tool. For example, if we pilot a new activity, we can count how many students persist in finishing this course compared with past courses. Some evidence is easily measured, such as student retention rates in a course, scores on pre- and post-assessments, and success on exit tickets. However, other data are more challenging to measure, for instance, student attitudes, student engagement, the quality of student interactions, or the tone in a classroom. Still, with the appropriate instruments, these can be measured. As an example, I integrate several strategies to promote positive learning mindsets into all aspects of my instruction in every course. To evaluate whether there are shifts in student beliefs and mindsets, I use pre- and post-mindset surveys. These survey data are useful for assessing whether my approach was effective in fostering positive academic mindsets.

Sometimes instructors triangulate both easily measurable data and more subjective data like observations. For example, imagine that you wanted to know whether the group-learning activities you introduced this semester were improving student learning outcomes. Maybe you noticed that a few more students:

- came to office hours
- came to class early to engage with you or their peers
- commented that they liked the group-work a lot
- used higher-level academic vocabulary
- asked more probing questions
- showed more visual representations on their tests
- scored higher on parts of the grading rubric that evaluated critical thinking skills

All of these data points suggest that the group-work is an effective addition to instruction. Other easily measured data are:

- student completion rates in the course
- quiz and exam scores
- frequency of student-to-student interactions about material
- frequency of academic vocabulary in conversations and writing
- number of students on-task during random checks

Some less easily measured data are:

- improved classroom vibe or tone
- improved students' positive feelings and attitudes
- increase in number of spontaneous utterances (e.g., "I have never been so challenged by a teacher")
- shifts in depth of questions about content
- increase in student comfort with mistakes, false starts, and taking risks
- shifts toward more sustained, in-depth arguments about the material, approaches, opinions, or reasoning

Data can be easy or difficult to measure. Still, instructors can triangulate evidence of student learning to engage in the continuous cycle of instruction improvement to assess whether a certain activity, strategy, or approach improves student outcomes.

Use Caution with Student Evaluations

Instructor-authored student evaluations are useful for looking at specific feedback on an activity or an instructional approach. However, there are issues with using standard student evaluations to assess instruction. First, students with more extreme views tend to write evaluations, as is apparent at ratemyteachers.com. Therefore, instructors are not receiving a representative sample of feedback from their students. Second, gender and ethnic/racial biases are evident in student evaluation responses (Huston, 2006; MacNell, Driscoll, & Hunt, 2015). Finally, researchers found no significant correlation between high scores on the standard teaching evaluations and improved student learning outcomes (Uttl, White, & Wong Gonzalez, 2017). Still, developing your own evaluations can be useful to solicit fine-grained data to inform the cycle of instruction improvement.

The following are two examples of specific mini-evaluations that instructors have used to refine their instruction. First, Dr. Claude Goldenberg used student evaluations in a way that built a community of learners, helped him to authentically solicit feedback, and improved his instruction. While he used this type of evaluation with doctoral students at Stanford, I have used it successfully with community college students. Claude's students responded to a mid-semester evaluation that he crafted with the intent of improving instruction. It included five "I agree" to "I disagree" statements on a five-point Likert scale. He included statements like "The lecture was useful"; "The peer writing evaluation activity was useful"; and "Working in groups was useful." Students responded how much they agreed or disagreed with those statements. Also, they could write comments in the space provided. Claude would collate all feedback and comments and debrief with his students in a meaningful way during the following class. He would project the responses in a PowerPoint presentation and facilitate a large-group discussion. Students felt heard, and he refined his instruction correspondingly.

The second is a mini-evaluation that can be used to solicit feedback about an entire class session or a specific activity. I encountered it in a Design Thinking course at Stanford. Students are given these sentence starters: "I liked . . . ," "I wish . . . ," and "What if . . . ?" At the end of a class, the students write their responses to these three prompts and/or share them orally. The instructor models it first. For example, if an instructor just taught a class where she piloted a peer-review-of-written-work activity, she could model, "I liked . . . that we worked in groups." "I wish . . . we had had more time to look at everybody's work in the group." "What if . . . next time, we have the peer-review rubric available to us ahead of time?" These two alternatives to the standard evaluation are ways to gather meaningful student feedback to refine instruction.

This chapter discussed educators as experts and improvisational artists who draw from well-elaborated schemas to create instruction, and as researchers who experiment with different instructional approaches in order to improve student outcomes. Instructors engage in the continuous cycle of instruction improvement by piloting strategies, gathering evidence about how impactful these strategies are for students, interpreting how these data can inform instruction, and ultimately refining instruction. There is a wide variety of data or evidence of student learning. Some data are easily measurable; and others are not. In later chapters, I discuss how instructors can draw from their schemas to create asset-based instruction where students' unique approaches and perspectives are illuminated and leveraged to unleash the learning potential of all students.

CHAPTER 2

Community College Students
Their Stories, Challenges, and Resilience

> To be true allies of students of color, students with disabilities, LGBTQ+
> students, and first-generation college students, instructors must do the
> daily work of leaning in and listening to the voices of people from back-
> grounds radically different than our own.

Community colleges play a key role in the U.S. postsecondary education system. They afford students who may not otherwise attain a 4-year
degree the extra support and resources they need to earn one, and they
offer a wide range of technical and professional certificates and associate's
degrees. Community college students are diverse and bring a wealth of
cultural assets to our classrooms. This chapter describes the problems
community colleges face in order to introduce the idea that instructors can be part of the solution if they implement inclusive, equitable,
inquiry-based instruction. Also, this chapter illustrates some challenges of
community college students in order to foster a sense of empathy about
their struggles and an appreciation of their resilience.

There are 1,103 community colleges in the United States, with 12
million students attending them. While 41% of all U.S. undergraduates
start in community college, unfortunately many never attain a 2-year degree—never mind a bachelor's degree. This is a problem as community
college students with a 2-year degree can earn an average of $5,400 per
year more than those who fail to attain one (Bailey, Belfield, & Benson,
2015). Consequently, in 2012, the 21st-Century Commission on the
Future of Community Colleges put out a call to U.S. community colleges to increase completion rates by 50% before the year 2020 (American
Association of Community Colleges [AACC], 2018). Before I discuss
classroom-level solutions to redressing this issue, this chapter describes
two challenges community colleges need to address in order to improve
retention, completion, and transfer rates of students. This chapter also
provides a window into the lives of some of our community college students in order to generate insight about instructional solutions.

CHALLENGES COMMUNITY COLLEGES FACE

The first challenge community colleges face is to improve the college skills of students, skills that some students have acquired before entry but many have not or have only partially acquired. A gap exists between the skills that graduating high school seniors possess and the skills incoming college students must possess to be successful in community college. College readiness includes study skills, soft skills, and prerequisite content knowledge and skills. One consequence of a lack of college readiness is that almost 70% of community college students place into developmental courses. Some institution-level solutions for improving college readiness are collaborations between P–16 partners, multiple-measure placement tests, accelerated developmental courses, and co-requisite courses. An example of a co-requisite course is a one-unit support course that students are required to take simultaneously with a five-unit, transfer-level English composition course. This support course redresses gaps in knowledge by teaching study, college, and grammar skills.

The second challenge community colleges face is that they need to bolster the success of those students who historically have been underrepresented among those with 4-year degrees. These include students of color, first-generation college students, students from low-income backgrounds, formerly incarcerated students, students in recovery, bilingual students, LGBTQ+ students, and students with learning disabilities. While about 20% of White and Asian students who begin at community colleges earn a bachelor's degree, only about 10% of Black or Hispanic students earn a bachelor's degree. Only 41% of students with learning disabilities who enroll in 2-year colleges actually graduate (Newman, Wagner, Cameto, & Knokey, 2009). Also, only 20% of first-generation college students obtain a 4-year degree within 10 years of their sophomore year of high school, compared with 42% of students who have at least one parent with a 4-year degree (Redford & Mulvaney Hoyer, 2017). One final statistic is that about one-third of community college students have household income levels below $20,000 and one-third work 35 hours or more each week. Consequently, there are many campus-wide programs that coordinate economic, health, and academic support services for students.

Teachin' It! provides classroom-level solutions to these two challenges. First, it offers strategies that redress the wide range of gaps in content knowledge and college skills in community college classrooms while simultaneously holding all students to the same high standards.

Second, it describes instruction that disrupts systemic inequity at the classroom level and equalizes the playing field for students from backgrounds that historically have been underrepresented among those with 4-year degrees.

STUDENT IDENTITIES, BACKGROUNDS, AND INTERSECTIONALITY

Before we continue, I would like to explain four assumptions made about student identity in this book. First, ethnic/racial or cultural groups are not monolithic. There are vast variations within each group. Second, students simultaneously maintain multiple identities and these identities may be fluid. For example, a student may identify as a first-generation college student (first-gen) *and* transgender *and* Asian *and* Latinx *and* formerly incarcerated. Another student might identify as African American *and* homosexual at age 18, and then at age 24 transition to identify as biracial and bisexual. Third, there is no one-size-fits-all, prescriptive instructional approach for any particular ethnic/racial or socioeconomic group, or any subgroup of students. Fourth, many more identities and cultural groups exist than those represented in this book.

The confluence of multiple identities that historically have been marginalized can contribute to extra risk factors for community college students. This is called intersectionality, the cumulative effects of overlapping or interdependent forms of discrimination and disadvantage, including gender identity, parent education status, income, sexuality, disability status, and ethnicity/race. For example, the Temple University/University of Wisconsin national study found that 42% of community college students indicate they have been "food insecure" and 46% report having been "housing insecure" (Goldrick-Rab, Richardson, Schneider, Hernandez, & Cady, 2018). However, the study found that Latinx, African American, and LGBTQ+ students, and students formerly in foster care experience higher rates of food and housing insecurity. In another example, 27% of first-gen students come from households making $20,000 or less, compared with 6% of college students with at least one parent with a 4-year degree (Redford & Mulvaney Hoyer, 2017). This contributes to 54% of first-gen students not completing their degrees, because they cannot afford to finish. First-gen students' risks for failing to complete their degrees are even higher if they identify with or are from the cultural groups mentioned earlier.

COMMUNITY COLLEGE STUDENTS: STORIES FROM THE EDGE

While this book highlights an asset-based model of instruction that builds on students' strengths, classroom instruction can be improved if it is informed by knowledge of the intimate challenges that community college students overcome to learn in our classrooms. This section offers an up-close and personal look into the lives of several community college students. In this chapter and throughout the book, students' names and other identifying details have been changed to guarantee anonymity. In each case below, the grade that the student earned is noted at the end because the achievement of a good grade despite great odds bespeaks the high levels of motivation, fierce tenacity, and resilience that community college students often bring to the classroom.

Salma Malik is a 20-year-old international student from Pakistan. She works hard in class, is quiet in groups, has a B average on tests, and has a part-time job. She shares a wealth of information about the food and culture from different regions of Pakistan and India. One day she was crying and talking on the phone outside of class. Her car insurance bill was out earlier on her desk. I figured, "Maybe her parents are mad at her for not paying her car insurance bill." I stepped outside of the class while students were working on independent work and asked what was wrong. She gushed, "My mother died 10 years ago and I live with my dad, stepmother, and three brothers. My parents ordered me to do an arranged marriage, but I do not want to." She continued, "I have to do what my parents say, because my two brothers will murder me if I don't." I walked her over to mental health services. Psychological services and the campus police worked with her to help resolve the safety issues with her family. She finished the course with a B+.

Valerie Jackson is a 19-year-old African American student who works part-time and was raised in foster care. She consistently contributes in class, asks lots of probing questions, has an 88% average, does well on tests, but has some missing homework assignments. One day it was 53 degrees in our classroom because the furnace broke and she was uncharacteristically short with me. Immediately, I thought that she must have been homeless before. I, too, was triggered by the cold in the classroom that day because I had spent time in my adult life being cold and lacking adequate shelter. On another day, Valerie missed two classes. I called and emailed her. She did not respond, so I notified the student intervention team. She got back in touch with me: "My friend lost their apartment in a fire. My car and my friend's couch are my only places to sleep . . . so, I had to go move with them." She had a new number and I suspected she did not have her own phone.

On Valerie's second day back to class, a dark cloud came over her, because she had done the wrong makeup quiz and had wasted her time. She cried in my office, "My friend committed suicide and we're not allowed to tell anyone." As we walked the .3 mile over to mental health services, she communicated a flurry of facts. In an almost cheerful tone, she told me that she was living some nights in her car and on her friend's couch, and sometimes she took showers at her former foster home. "When it is really cold, I can't sleep in my car, because it costs too much to pay for gas to run my car all night." She said this all matter-of-factly, like she did not really know that she was homeless. She must have seen the concern on my face because she started to reassure me, "Don't worry, Mrs. Darling. I have learned how to live on less food." All of a sudden her small stature became apparent to me. She was clearly under 100 pounds and barely 5 feet tall—exuding pride, optimism, coping strategies, and masked desperation. I walked her over to psychological services. She got a B+.

Ashley Tinder is White and 36 years old. She works part-time, attends school full-time, has perfect attendance and homework completion, experiences test anxiety, and is working on developing stronger growth mindset talk about her math ability. She has given birth three times. One baby died at birth. One was adopted by a family member, and she is not allowed contact. She is married and has a 2-year-old daughter for whom she would do anything. She is working toward a nursing degree. She was addicted to meth for 4 years and was in and out of prison for felony convictions for 8 years. She has not used crystal meth for over 2 years. She is active in the group for students who formerly have been incarcerated. She got an A.

Franklin Bearsay is White and 18 and this is his first semester of college. He is studying to become a firefighter. He is the youngest of three siblings. He works full-time, goes to school full-time, raises his hand a lot, and is eager to ask any question to help him learn better in class. He is rapidly building strong study skills, contributes a lot in groups, and is developing an identity as a competent adult learner. Last year he fled from his family's home in a rural town, because his parents and siblings "were all doing drugs." He told me, "My 20-year-old brother died from fentanyl overdose 3 months ago." Therefore, he moved in with his aunt and uncle next to his community college, a county away from his home town, in order to begin classes. He passed his driving test during his first semester of college. He got a B.

Sam Siengthai is 29 and was born in Thailand. He wants to be an EMT. He lived in a Thai refugee camp before he came to the United States as a teen. He is working toward becoming a U.S. citizen. He works really hard both inside and outside of class, has an A average, and leads a study group with three recent high school graduates from this class. He works almost full-time and goes to school full-time. I credit the success of this particular section of my class to his leadership and his instilling the desire to learn in the other students in the class. He is confident and comfortable taking risks in class and making mistakes. He always offers to present at the whiteboard—especially when other students are reticent. He performs well on all assessments. He got an A.

Lisette Echevarria is a Latinx math student who does well on assessments, but has spotty attendance. About midway in the semester, she had an A average, but missed two classes in a row. I emailed her to say, "You can still pass this class if you come in to take the test on Wednesday." She showed up on Wednesday and told me that she had written me a long email, but then she deleted it. I said, "Even a bad email is communication, and bad communication is better than no communication." As we walked together toward class, she explained, "What I was going to write is that I am the oldest of seven children, and my mother is a single parent and unemployed. We are homeless. It is hard for me to come to class, finish this course, or even my degree, because of my family responsibilities." She failed the class that semester, because she stopped coming to class.

Many community college instructors have seen students with similar stories sitting in their classrooms. It is humbling to consider the challenges that these students have overcome in order to learn. Instructors recognizing symptoms of distress and speaking to students, directing them to student services as needed, and simply showing by their interest that they care, can contribute in the end to the success of these students.

The Beast Called Poverty

I share the following piece I wrote about my own life to help instructors experience the world through the eyes of a first-gen college student living in poverty.

> Poverty stalks you, like a monster, like a legion of zombies, like the devil—waiting for a moment of vulnerability so it can close in and snatch your soul. Even if you have enough to eat, you are always one root canal, one car repair, one misunderstanding at work, one injury away from financial catastrophe. The world does not look kindly on you either, so you are

haunted by shame and isolation, too. A decade of struggling on the brink leaves you living off the fumes of hope. You stand, petrified, knee-deep in terror, scared that the pain in your molar will turn into an abscess that you can't afford to fix. You're afraid that the knocking beneath the hood of your car signals the loss of your sole means of transportation. You recall 6 weeks last winter when you didn't have a car, and you lived 10 miles from the nearest store. You had to walk to work and beg rides for your child to go to school when it was 40 degrees (Fahrenheit) below zero. You swallow your words at work when your boss sexually harasses you, because even 5 days without pay could leave you and your child without a home. You frequent thrift stores looking for treasures. That, at least, is a pleasure. You feel trapped in your pained body. The chronic stress of living in poverty creates the fertile ground for persistent and elusive pain and health issues. Sometimes you are drowning in hopelessness and you go numb for a few days—or a week. You are a lifeless corpse, floating down the river, waiting to bump into a log . . . so at least then you will know that you are still alive. Other times, despair unleashes your festering rage that leaks like corrosive acid onto those for whom you are entrusted to care—then the guilt sets in. Although you have friends who are also poor, still, you feel alone. Generous strangers save you when you face homelessness and they give you a place to stay, for a while. Other times, you have enough resources and are able to maintain a stable place, for a while . . . until that monster called poverty gets you into its sights. Like an extra in a horror movie, you sense escape is futile. You scramble through the woods screaming, only to twist your ankle and fall at the last moment, inevitably swallowed by that beast called poverty.

Byron Reaves: Once a First-Gen Student, Now a First-Gen Mentor

In this section my colleague Byron Reaves discusses part of his own journey from being a first-gen, African American student to attaining his master's degree in Counseling to coordinating the award-winning Student Success Program at Santa Rosa Junior College. In this role, Byron built and oversees a dynamic, multicultural student success team that provides peer mentoring and student support. Byron is also the Mentor Coordinator for UMOJA, a campus-based learning community that supports African American college students. In addition, Byron is an equity consultant who has helped me to make my instruction more inclusive and equitable. Part of Byron's mission involves supporting the success of all students— with a particular focus on African American students. He draws faculty, administration, and students into the conversation of how to change the

larger system to make it more equitable, more welcoming, and fairer for
students who sometimes are left out. What follows is an excerpt from an
interview with Byron about his story.

New Haven is one of the more dire cities on the East Coast . . . a couple
of years ago, it was one of the most dangerous cities in the U.S. It is just
like any other inner city. It is a rough place so I came up with very limited
resources. My mom and dad worked hard to move us out. So ok cool. I
went to high school at Hamden High and there I was, a struggling student.
I have four brothers in total but my two older brothers, they struggled to
find their way. They were kind of caught up in the streets. And so, I didn't
really have community examples, other than my mom and dad, to look up
to . . . to say . . . "Oh, I can do this, that, or that." I just kind of went to the
streets and figured out my life. I got a scholarship to [Albertus Magnus]
College for basketball. The situation did not work out.

I was working real hard, working overnight, and I got all Fs. I dropped
out my first semester at Albertus Magnus with all Fs . . . mainly because I
didn't feel like it was a place for me to be . . . it was an all-White, Catholic
Church college. Yeah, I didn't connect with any of the instructors but I
had a sister, Sister Gil Mary. . . . And I will never forget, she saved my life,
eventually. She kept calling me. She said, "Byron, come back." I was like,
"No, no, no, no. I'm not going back!" Later on she kept calling me and
eventually I went back to [college]. She kept calling me and calling. . . .
And later on in life, even, she kept calling me. That Sister [saw] something
in me that I didn't see.

[Another thing] that brought me back [to college] was that I was
working at Walmart at night and I wanted a manager job and it was a couple
dollars more and the person who got the manager job was a complete you
know . . . not a good person. And with that being said that person got the job
over me. I was like, "Why?" They were like, "He has a degree."

. . . And so, my first semester again, this time at Livingstone College
in North Carolina; it was a HBCU [historically Black college or university],
an all-Black college. I got all As there. Now, I don't know how I got all As,
right, but I connected with the instructors. You know they were Black. All
Black instructors. They gave us real-world scenarios and they applied that
to the curriculum they taught.

For Byron, having Sister Gil Mary calling him and believing in him
was a game-changer for his educational success. I told Byron, "I have a
few African American students in my classes, but I do not allow them to

fail. I call them if they stop coming to class." Byron said, "The students you call will remember that for years down the road." During Byron's master's degree journey, one of his instructors used "wise feedback," which is explained in Chapter 3. She gave ample critical feedback, held Byron to the same high standards as everyone else, and communicated, "I believe you can do it."

> So, what was important for me was that I went to my master's program, right? I had never done APA. And I had an instructor [who expected] that writing format. It was an issue. Like, she literally ripped my paper apart, and there was more red than black, and right away when she gave it back to me she said, "I'm gonna give this back to you and let you see it. But I want you to come in right after class." She spent 45 minutes with me and she changed the outlook of my whole master's program. Right. Forty-five minutes with me. It told me that [her feedback] was not a penalty against me . . . and it was not held against me . . . that it did not say that I did not know what I was doing. It wasn't a marker of how smart you are, right? It just validated that this is a difficult thing and you can make it through it and I'm going to help you. It was a feeling. There's a trust, and I'm sure the research is out there, that African American students . . . we instinctively think [or] feel whether we belong here or somebody wants to help us . . . genuinely. Right. . . . And, so for me, in that master's program that was it. It was like, "Oh you want me to succeed!" You're like, Okay, let's tune in for 45 minutes. Boom, boom, boom.

This underlines the importance of genuinely communicating that you believe in a student as well as holding the student to high standards while giving critical feedback. Students who historically have been disenfranchised from the advantages that a system potentially affords are savvy. They can sense when an instructor genuinely wants them to succeed. It builds trust. In this next excerpt, Byron talks about African American students he mentors currently in his role as student success coordinator.

> Students who seek support may feel like, "You're judging me, right?" Just because of the stereotype we're talking about—the stereotype of a Black person—needs extra help or more help. Right? So, what I hear from our [African American] students all the time—is they say, "Well I don't want to seem like a charity case. Maybe I need help, but I also don't want to seem like I'm stupid. I'm just not prepared yet to do the work that I need to do."

This response underscores an important point. Students of color, first-gen students, or students with few resources are proud and independent. They have had to rely on themselves to overcome challenging circumstances and systemic inequities. Therefore, it is important to mentor them in ways that dignify them.

In conclusion, instruction can play a role in improving retention and transfer rates of students. However, community college instructors face unique challenges in addressing varying degrees of college readiness and redressing systemic inequity at the classroom level. Many community college students have multiple challenges that increase their risk of not attaining 4-year degrees. They may identify with several marginalized cultural groups, which in turn magnifies their risk due to intersectionality. They may have experiences with incarceration, discrimination, substance issues, poverty, family obligations, trauma, or disabilities. There is no one-size-fits-all strategy for community college students. However, as we saw from Byron's example, reaching out, leaning in, and listening can go a long way toward bolstering student success.

CHAPTER 3

Instructor and Student Mindsets That Bolster Student Success

> The greatest act of social justice an instructor can commit is to create safe learning environments where students from all backgrounds and identities can actualize their full potential as powerful learners.

This chapter is about disrupting systemic inequity at the classroom level. "Systemic inequity" is created when institutional, social, and economic systems perpetuate discrimination and bias against particular groups of people, thus creating barriers to their success. For example, in some states K–12 school funding is linked to the taxes collected in the neighborhood of each school, thus ensuring that students from more affluent neighborhoods have more per-pupil funding and access to better schooling. This systemic inequity perpetuates a cycle that prevents students from lower-resource neighborhoods from having equal access to educational opportunities. It is a discriminatory system that perpetuates and preserves inequity. Here are two other examples of systemic inequity. First, Black teen defendants in court are awarded more jail time for the same offenses as White teen defendants (Spohn, 2000; Starr & Rehavi, 2012). As a second example, institutional inequity is embedded in some U.S. policing and court systems in regions where police officers are more likely to stop and search Black residents, even though Blacks are less likely to be carrying contraband than Whites (U.S. Department of Justice, 2015).

As college instructors we are uniquely positioned to disrupt systemic and institutional inequity at the classroom level. We are potential agents of change for our students of color and other historically marginalized groups. Instructors can work toward not replicating the systems of inequity that operate outside of our classrooms. We can ensure that our classes provide equal opportunities for all students to excel. This chapter offers powerful, practical ideas that redress systemic inequity at the classroom level and equalize the playing field for all students. It is divided into three sections. The first section describes leveraging instructor mindsets to foster equitable classrooms. The second section discusses how to foster a growth mindset classroom that bolsters learning for all students. The third section demonstrates how to alleviate stereotype threat and mentor students from backgrounds that are radically different than one's own.

INSTRUCTOR BELIEFS AND AN EQUITY MINDSET

As noted in Chapter 1, instructors draw from a complicated schema to create instruction. While content knowledge and instructional knowledge are components of an educator's schema, so are instructor beliefs, attitudes, and mindsets. These beliefs are communicated through feedback, praise, instructor–student interactions, classroom norms, tone, curriculum choices, and other instructor moves. Beliefs inform classroom practices that either optimize or undermine student success. As instructors seeking to refine our practices to improve learning outcomes for all students, we engage in the cycle of instruction improvement.

Because instructors are less diverse than community college students, frequently we teach and mentor students from backgrounds different than our own. While over half of community college students are non-White, only 25% of community college faculty are non-White (AACC, 2018). Also, it is likely that the majority of instructors are not first-generation college students nor have they lived in poverty.

Many of our beliefs may be implicit. Although we strive to have an equity mindset, instructors are human and possess beliefs and implicit biases that may interfere with serving students who have lived experiences radically different than our own. An implicit bias is a stereotype that is unconscious; we may not know that we have it. Drawing from Piaget's theory of assimilation and accommodation, sometimes instructors have components of their schemas that do not serve all students equally well. They may need to accommodate new ideas in order to adapt their schemas to cultivate an equity mindset. Cultivating an equity mindset is a lifelong journey. To take Harvard's implicit bias test as part of that endeavor, go to implicit.harvard.edu/implicit/takeatest.html. Black/White and old/young tests have been piloted and refined for a longer period of time than the others on the site, so I would try those first.

Several studies underscore the importance of instructor bias. For example, campuses where there is discourse around blaming students for their failures tend to have increased numbers of lower-performing students (Diamond, 2008). When faculty say things like "Our students will never be able do that," and "Poor students do badly, because they come from families that do not value college," it takes the burden off the instructors to change their own instruction and places it firmly on the backs of the students.

Other research indicates that when instructors have differentiated expectations for students from different ethnic, racial, or class backgrounds, it undermines minority student success. Several studies have indicated that when educators have higher expectations for middle-class White students than for students of color or low-income students, the achievement gap widens in those classrooms (McKown & Weinstein, 2008; Van den Bergh, Denessen, Hornstra, Voeten, & Holland, 2010). These expectations are communicated in instructor behaviors such as negative or positive speech toward students, quality and number of instructor–student interactions, or who is called on to answer questions. For my master's degree, 25 years ago, I videotaped and tracked my student–teacher interactions. I found that I had longer and more frequent interactions with male students. In effect, males received more one-on-one instruction time with the instructor, which is a valued classroom currency. Now, I am very conscious of tracking my classroom interactions. I try to talk to every student every day and hold all students equally accountable for presenting their reasoning in class.

Pronouncing students' names correctly, meeting students in one's office, and shaking students' hands on the first day of class are all behaviors that communicate, "I like you." These are microaffirmations, which are little behaviors that communicate, "I am sure about you." These create equal opportunities for all students. However, not remembering or mispronouncing specific students' names, not holding all students to the same high standards, having different expectations for different students, interacting with some students less than others, and not calling on students equally are all behaviors that communicate, "I am not sure about you." These are microaggressions, behaviors that communicate negative feelings about students, which undermine students' sense of belonging and therefore demotivate them. Examining our implicit biases, differential expectations, and classroom practices can help us to cultivate an equity mindset to serve all students equally.

FOSTERING A GROWTH MINDSET CLASSROOM

This section focuses on implementing growth mindset strategies (Dweck, 2006, 2007) that are framed with an equity mindset. It illustrates strategies for cultivating a classroom environment where all students feel safe to experiment, take risks, make mistakes, and explore in order to become competent learners. This section is not about teaching grit or teaching students to work harder. Students who have overcome issues related to incarceration, discrimination, sexual abuse, substance abuse, or poverty already possess grit.

Furthermore, telomere research explains why instructors should not focus primarily on emphasizing grit and effort, but instead should remove barriers for students. A telomere is a protective casing at the end of each strand of our DNA (Figure 3.1). Telomeres are indicators of aging. As we age, our telomeres naturally shorten, and shortened telomeres predict greater incidences of disease and an earlier death. Exposure to chronic stress can precipitate the shortening of telomeres (Mathur et al., 2016). Recent studies indicate that the telomeres of students who are either Black or who have lived in poverty are shorter than those of students who are White or middle-class (Geronimus et al., 2015). Researchers speculate that the shorter telomeres are due to the fact that Black students are chronically exposed to the stress of systemic racism (Lee, Kim, & Neblett, 2017) and poor students have been exposed to the chronic stress of housing insecurity, food insecurity, and other factors associated with poverty. The bottom line is that there are measurable, physical costs for students who navigate a system with built-in barriers to success: shorter telomeres. What is even more disturbing is that Black or poor students who are the high achievers in their families have even shorter telomeres than their lower-achieving siblings (Miller, Yu, Chen, & Brody, 2015). This is not true for affluent and White students. This means that although students who achieve against all odds are to be commended, they do so at a great physical cost. Therefore, teaching marginalized students to work harder is not a great strategy. However, disrupting systemic inequity at the classroom level is a high-impact strategy, because it actually alleviates barriers that high-achieving poor and Black students face. On the positive side, studies indicate that alleviating chronic stress can attenuate the damage to—although not repair—telomeres.

Growth mindset theory (Dweck, 2006, 2007) has been misapplied and misappropriated in K–14 classrooms to the degree that it may be useful to just go ahead and use a different word for it. Let us define

Figure 3.1. Telomeres

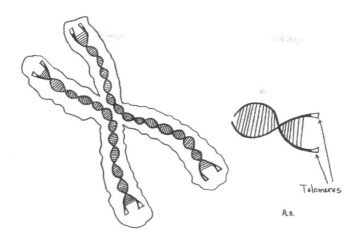

it, though. Growth mindset describes an implicit theory of intelligence, our underlying, core beliefs about whether or not intelligence can be changed. In incremental theory, now called *growth mindset*, individuals believe that their ability or intelligence can be improved over time—even if they begin at a low level of performance. Intelligence can grow. For example, "I can get better at technology if I apply myself and learn some new strategies." In entity theory, now called *fixed mindset*, individuals believe that their ability or intelligence cannot be changed; that their ability is innate. Intelligence and ability are fixed. For example, "I am not a math person."

Another important point to remember about growth mindset is that it is contextual. No one is "a growth mindset person." That would represent an entity theory approach or a fixed mindset. For example, a specific person could possess a growth mindset about learning languages, but have a fixed mindset about learning writing. Individuals could believe that they are just not music people, so they will never be able to play the piano (a fixed mindset). However, they may believe that they can become better writers, because they understand that a writer is someone who works hard, struggles, learns new strategies, and gets better over time (a growth mindset).

Not only is a growth mindset contextual, but the degree of the growth mindset in an area can wax and wane depending on how much it is fostered. For example, when I got my PhD at Stanford, I was 54, but the median age of my cohort was 28. These students had growth mind-sets in terms of using technology, but I did not. I worked hard over the 5 years to develop a growth mindset in terms of technology. I am successful to a large degree with that. However, sometimes I backslide and when faced with a technological challenge like the online component of a course, for example, my growth mindset with regard to technology needs a little pep talk. Carol Dweck told an audience at Stanford that for some students a "light" immediately goes on, but for other students it can take time to convince them about the merits of a growth mindset. From my experiences teaching students, I find that the longer the history of "failure" in math, the more motivated students are to adopt a growth mindset in math. Still, I notice that some students require more conversations and convincing than others.

Several studies found that when students possess growth mindsets they perform better in math, science, and English (Boaler, 2016; Good, Aronson, & Inzlicht, 2003; Aronson, Fried, & Good, 2002). In addition, several studies have found that when growth mindset interventions are used and students shift their mindsets toward a growth mindset, then their achievement improves, sometimes for years after the short intervention (Blackwell, Trzesniewski, & Dweck, 2007; Boaler, 2016). The following four messages are communicated in all growth mindset interventions: (1) all mathematicians, scientists, physicists, or writers struggle to be good at their crafts; (2) mistakes, revisions, drafts, exploring, taking risks, and experimenting are all a natural part of the learning process and building new neural connections; (3) expending effort while engaging in challenging, complex tasks forms new neural connections and creates brain plasticity, and if a task is difficult, it does not mean that we are not "good" at it; and (4) we can get better at anything by expending effort and developing new strategies.

It seems simple enough, right? The challenge is to adapt our schemas to accommodate these ideas and weave these strands through all aspects of our instruction. In the following paragraphs, I discuss four instructional domains through which instructors can draw these growth mindset strands. They are *classroom norms, feedback, assessments*, and *group-worthy tasks*.

Norms

Growth mindset norms value mistakes, false paths, the process, taking risks, drafts, revisions, productive struggle, and effort. Norms communicate that making mistakes, experimenting, negotiating, understanding, arguing, and exploring are key ways to engage in the process of learning. They communicate that if something is hard, it does not mean that you are not good at it. On the contrary, struggling and expending effort are natural parts of learning and create greater neural connections. In general, norms should emphasize the process and not the destination. Also, growth mindset norms communicate that all experts make a lot of mistakes and struggle on their journey to becoming experts. Norms should communicate that unique approaches are valued. Finally, norms should emphasize that students in the room are practitioners in the field. A community of learners, in terms of growth mindset, could be a community of practitioners. Students could be considered budding physicists, mathematicians, biologists, historians, or writers. Developing norms together is a powerful approach to ensuring that growth mindset norms inform classroom learning.

Feedback, Praise, Questions

Growth mindset feedback, praise, and questions can be used at the classroom level to redress the achievement gap for ethnic/racial and linguistic minority students and first-generation college students (Mueller & Dweck, 1998). One goal of growth mindset praise is to help students embrace productive struggling. Carol Dweck, in "The Perils and Promises of Praise" (2007), cautions against telling students they are "brilliant" or "smart" when they get correct answers or good grades. Instead she advocates praising the process, effort, and incremental growth. Instead of saying, "Wow! You got an A on that quiz. You are really smart in bio!" one could say, "Wow! You must have worked hard studying for that bio quiz. You must have developed some strong study strategies and also spent a lot of time learning the material!" Similarly, Jo Boaler (2016) recommends that instructors focus on the process of learning and the value of productive struggle rather than on academic performance and correct answers in classrooms. Posted on Boaler's YouCubed site are eight teaching practices that *block* productive struggle. Among them are: "praising students for their smarts," "calling on students who know the correct answer," and communicating that it is okay to "not be a math person." Dweck's poster listing eight habits that *promote* productive struggle suggests "praising students for perseverance." Tables 3.1, 3.2, 3.3 are examples of feedback and questions that I use every day in class to foster a growth mindset classroom. These ideas were gleaned and refined from

Table 3.1. Use Probing Questions

Instead of asking this . . .	One could ask . . .
What is the correct answer or solution?	Why do you agree or disagree with that approach or way of thinking?
What is the right approach?	What assumptions are you making when you approach it that way?
How many people got _____ for an answer?	Could you tell me a little bit more about what you were thinking here?

Table 3.2. Praise the Process and Skill Development

Instead of saying this . . .	One could say . . .
See, you are good at English. You got an A on your last test.	Great job! You must have worked really hard to improve your skills. Maybe you can share your study strategies with the class.
I am sorry to see that you got a D on your anatomy exam. At least you are good at writing.	Can you identify which skills you need to improve? What other study strategies could you use next time?
You got it! I told you that you were smart.	You studied hard for your English test and your improved knowledge and skills are reflected in your grade.

Table 3.3. Praise Mistakes and "Aha" Moments

If a student says . . .	An instructor can respond . . .
I can't write an essay. I keep messing up. This is my third attempt at the first paragraph.	This looks like a pretty demanding topic. What would a focused first, second, or third try look like?
I give up. I will never be able to write a comparative essay.	You may not have the skills to do it—YET. What strategies have you already tried?
I keep making mistakes. I am not a science person. No one in my family is a science person.	Can you tell me about an "aha" moment today, where you learned from a mistake, misleading assumption, or false path you went down?

reading a lot of Dweck's work, teaching educators, and experimenting in the classroom.

To foster a growth mindset in my classroom, I frame successes and failures in terms of skill development. If a student gets a poor grade on a factoring quiz, I say, "It looks like you still need to work on those factoring skills." If a student says, "I can't do fractions," I reframe this, "Oh, you have not learned all the skills you need to add and subtract fractions, yet?" Conversely, if a student has all correct answers or gets an A, I say, "It looks like you invested a lot of time into learning those skills for that test. Can you share some of your strategies with our class?" This shifts the focus away from a fixed mindset, where students think they are naturally good or bad at math, toward a growth mindset, where students focus on the learning process and the skills needed to be successful on the journey to becoming competent math learners and mathematicians.

When students explain their reasoning on the board or in whole-group discussions, whether a student has the correct answer or not, I ask, "Could you tell us a little more about what you were thinking here?" When an instructor elicits student thinking, it shifts the focus away from the correctness of the student's answer toward the student's unique reasoning and approach and individual learning journey. In this way, students become comfortable with sharing their reasoning—even if they know they have an incorrect answer. They understand that sharing their mistakes and false paths will help them and other students have those "aha" moments. Also, it shifts the perception away from the teacher or textbook being the authority about math and toward the student's mathematical reasoning being the guiding force. I notice which strategies students are using and comment on them as I walk around the room, too. "You drew a diagram to explain your reasoning," or "Your organization skills are really strong." How do you communicate to your students that mistakes, false paths, and first tries are a crucial part of the learning process? How do you communicate that their skill development is an important part of learning?

Assessments

Assessments that allow for revisions and emphasize the draft quality of assignments and solutions are a great way of communicating that mistakes are sources of learning. Instead of allowing students to drop their lowest quiz grade, allow them to retake that quiz. Also, instead of simply allowing them to drop their lowest homework grade, allow them to drop the lowest grade on homework that they actually submitted. Their lowest homework grade may be a zero, which reflects no effort. That way you are praising effort and emphasizing that learning is a process. I allow students to replace their lowest test score with their final exam score, if it is higher. I tell them, "If you did not master the content at the time of the test as indicated by the low score, then you can invest time after that to master the skills and it will be reflected on the cumulative final exam score." Also, I give exit tickets, quick assessments as students leave class. These are not graded, to emphasize that I am focused not just on performance, but also on the process of learning.

Tasks That Promote a Growth Mindset

Growth mindset tasks and activities should not move students toward one correct answer or one correct approach or method to solve a problem. They should be group-worthy and involve students working in groups to negotiate, compare, discuss, and co-construct knowledge. They should be open-ended, low-floor/high-ceiling tasks that invite experimentation and value students' unique approaches. They should be facilitated using probing, open-ended questions that further the co-construction of knowledge.

Launching a Growth Mindset Class

I recommend launching growth mindset activities on the first day of class to set the stage. Some things I do are: (1) show a video, provide an article, or show neuroscience slides on growth mindset; (2) share a personal growth mindset story; and (3) facilitate a powerful growth mindset activity.

I share examples of all three in this section. Showing a growth mindset video on the first day is a great way to launch your class. It might be a video by Carol Dweck or a video by Jo Boaler if it is a math or science class. Students can even pre-view or pre-read a video or an article before class. Then students can respond on the online forum to the prompt, "Name two ideas about growth mindset that can support your success this semester." If students read a growth mindset article in class, you can ask them to **jigsaw** read it, having different groups read and present on different parts of the article, or have all students read the entire article, but have different groups be the experts who present on assigned parts of the article. Sometimes I share images and research about neuroscience with students. For example, I share neuroscience slides illustrating that when students complete novel, challenging tasks it creates more neural connections, and that students who possess a growth mindset pay greater attention to their mistakes (Moser, Schroder, Heeter, Moran, & Lee, 2011). Also, I show a slide of a brain with a lot of neural activity and tell the story about Cameron. She is the 6-year-old girl who had the right hemisphere of her brain removed (a hemispherectomy), because she

Figure 3.2. Before I Discovered Growth Mindset

had seizures due to Rasmussen's encephalitis. Her left side was paralyzed. However, within weeks of working hard, she had grown new connections and recovered many of her left-side functions (Gibbon, 2015). Providing students with stories, research, and images is a powerful way to help them develop a growth mindset.

The second strategy is to share one of your own mindset stories. I share a story about my own struggles with fostering a growth mindset. I tell students about how when I went to Stanford, other students were wealthier and had come from Ivy League colleges like Harvard or Cornell. I am a first-generation college student and I graduated from an open-access state college. I tell my students, "My professor assigned a book review." I had thought a book review was the same as a book report. I explain the difference to my students: "Apparently, a book review is something that you get published. I spent 14 hours writing a book 'report.' I got a C−. Other students got As and said, 'It only took me 45 minutes.'" I tell my students, "I felt depressed and discouraged and began to question whether I was a writer or if I belonged in the PhD program." I show them Figure 3.2. I continue, "I heard Carol Dweck speak,

Figure 3.3. Five Years Later

and it inspired me to consciously foster a growth mindset about my writing. I worked hard. After thousands of hours of working in the writing center, three published articles, and a Fulbright scholarship, I wrote my first book" (Figure 3.3). I share this experience with students about how I struggled and failed at first. Also, this is a great time to explain that comparing yourself with others cements a fixed mindset. I explain, "Some students have more skills than you when they begin a course. Maybe they learned them already in an earlier class. It does not seem fair, but it is what it is. It is going to take you longer to learn topics and skills if you have not mastered those skills already. It does not mean you are not a writer, math person, science person, musician, etc."

The third strategy is a powerful activity I created called Finding Your Growth Mindset. I have used it in both Spanish and English with pre-college to doctorate-level students with much success. It can be done in any subject. In this activity, I give students an 8.5" x 11" sheet of paper and colored pencils, and post a PowerPoint slide asking them to *Draw a picture of something you are good at, something that you got better at over time by working hard.*

Students draw pictures of soccer, writing, debating, parenting, sewing, or guitar to illustrate the activity in which they have improved (Figure 3.4). It is remarkable that even when students say things like, "I can't draw," it is easy to discern what they draw. Maybe it's because they are drawing activities about which they feel passionate. I explain to them how this is one area in which they have a growth mindset, and that growth mindset is contextual and we do not have growth mindsets in all areas. Because I teach math to students who historically have not liked math, I connect this activity to math learning. After we go around the room and talk about what students have drawn, I ask them to respond to the following three sentence **starter frames** (sentence frames are a great way to scaffold any activity—particularly a new activity): (1) "When I make a mistake, I ____"; (2) "When it gets challenging, I ____"; and (3) "In order to get better at it, I ____." Students write down their answers and discuss them in groups, and we share out as a whole class. I scribe the class's responses to all three prompts in three columns on the whiteboard. Then students discuss in groups which of these strategies they could use in math class to foster a growth mindset. I take a picture of the whiteboard and post the strategies that we come up with on the course website. Students say things like:

When I make a mistake:
- I try to learn from it.
- I ask others for help.
- I think back to a similar situation or problem.
- I try again.

When it gets challenging:
- I take a break and then come back.
- I get help from the book or another person.
- I breathe.
- I yell.
- I persist.

In order to get better at it:
- I practice.
- I work hard.
- I keep trying; or
- I Google it.

We talk about building a growth mindset in math and how they can use these strategies to be successful in math if they actively cultivate a growth mindset.

Figure 3.4. Student Drawings from the First Day of Class

We come back to these drawings throughout the semester. One student, Luis, was struggling with math around the 7th week and was about to give up, because he was "not a math person." I said, "Well, what did you mention on the first day that you got better at?" He said, "I can't remember." I asked him, "What did you *draw?*" He immediately said, "Soccer." I said, "When you try to get a goal and you miss it, do you just drop the ball and say, 'Well, I guess soccer is not for me and jet out of there?' He said, "Of course not." While students do not remember what is said on the first day, they remember what they drew. This is a great example of how tapping into students' prior experiences and engaging them in complex tasks helps them to store concepts in their long-term memories, too. Luis was able to build on his understanding of growth mindset strategies in one area to foster his growth mindset in another area, math.

Fostering a growth mindset classroom is not something that you do only on the first day, however. Instructors must integrate growth mindset principles into all aspects of instruction throughout the semester. Having a bank of videos, articles, group-worthy tasks, and high-leverage growth mindset activities is a good idea. Check out www.feliciadarling.com to access vetted growth mindset videos, posters, and articles.

The Cycle of Instruction Improvement and Growth Mindset

Instructors can do pre- and post-surveys to see whether their growth mindset activities and strategies are effective. Many students jump right on the growth mindset bandwagon, while others take a long time to make that paradigm shift. Frequently, I spend extra time with a couple of students to support them. Besides my pre- and post-surveys, I look for keywords and behaviors to indicate that students have shifted toward a growth mindset. For example, are they anxious to get the correct answer? Are they using language like, "I can't write," or "I hate reading"? These words and behaviors communicate that the students have a fixed mindset. In a growth mindset classroom, students should feel safe experimenting, making mistakes, sharing their approaches, and taking risks. If students come to the board even when they are unsure whether their reasoning is "correct," that is a positive indicator. If students are engaging in arguments about concepts, approaches, and assumptions, then I feel like the class has made a shift toward having a growth mindset.

Two studies found that when instructors possess a growth mindset in their subject area, students benefit (Anderson, Boaler, & Dieckmann, 2018; Canning, Muenks, Green, & Murphy, 2019). If we cultivate a growth mindset about our skills at fostering a growth mindset classroom, we likely will get better with time. While growth mindset strategies, framed by an equity mindset, can do a lot to disrupt larger systemic inequity at the classroom level, many scholars caution that growth mindset strategies informed by implicit biases can perpetuate systemic inequity. This next section addresses this.

ALLEVIATING STEREOTYPE THREAT

Instructors ask, "How can I connect to and reach students who are from backgrounds other than my own?" "I come from a wealthy background; how can I be sensitive to my low-income students?" I am White, how can I mentor a student who is African American?" First, these are powerful questions to ask to disrupt systemic inequity. Second, instructors will need to experiment and expend effort to get better at mentoring over time.

Three topics predominate in stereotype threat intervention research: (1) stereotype bias; (2) stereotype threat interventions that improve achievement for females, students of color, and low-income students; and

(3) other equity moves that include how to mentor students from backgrounds different than those of the majority of instructors.

Stereotype Bias Defined

A stereotype is a preconceived idea that all the members of a group share certain characteristics. *Stereotype bias* is a tendency (frequently implicit) to dislike—or like—members of a particular group based on the stereotype. Stereotypes exist about every group. When we think of people in groups, stereotypes pop up. These may reflect implicit biases we have or just our knowledge of familiar societal stereotypes associated with these groups of people. Finish the following sentence starters:

     1. Homeless people _____
     2. Asian women _____
     3. Black men _____
     4. Obese people _____
     5. Poor people _____

     The following story illustrates what stereotype bias looks like in everyday life. I, a White woman wearing a blazer, was in a popular department store buying a karaoke machine. After 5 minutes of waiting in the photo department, I hopped behind the service counter and reached around the register to access the phone system to call the manager. Pretending I was an employee, I said, "We need someone down here in photo. We have a customer waiting." The responder said, "Okay." I said, "Thanks." The service counter is 15 feet from the "employees only" door. While I was behind the counter using the phone, several employees walked in or out of the employee door without giving me even a glance. I returned to the front of the service counter, but after another 5 minutes I called up front again, "We need help in photo." Again, a steady stream of employees walked in and out of the employee door. Eventually, a sales associate showed up and helped me with my request. Then I walked to the front of the store to wait in one of the six long checkout lines. I was behind a tall, soft-faced, Latinx customer of slight build, about 15 years old. He was holding his phone with his right hand looking at texts, a video, or something. His left hand was in his jeans pocket. A Latinx sales associate in his early 20s rushed over and whispered something in the customer's ear. Immediately, the Latinx customer slipped his hand out of his pocket.

I asked him, "What did that guy say to you?" "He said, 'Customers are getting scared, because you have your hand in your pocket. Could you take it out?'" I was all like, "What the f—? They can't say that to you. That's racist!" Being a blazer-wearing White woman, I was indignant and angry. The saddest part of the story was how the teen just kind of shrugged his shoulders and showed little outward signs of cognitive dissonance. He just reflexively complied in a business-as-usual-for-a-brown-skinned-male-buying-something manner.

This story underscores how different people's lived experiences in the United States are based on their ethnicity/race and socioeconomic status. I was afforded unearned status that would have allowed me to rob the photo department of a major department store, whereas a mother's gentle, brown-skinned son could have been shot by a bystander who imagined that he secretly had his fingers wrapped tightly around a gun or a knife in his pocket. That is stereotype bias—when someone imprints traits on a person from a particular group without having any inside information about who the person actually is.

Stereotype Threat Defined

Claude Steele, author of *Whistling Vivaldi* (2010), introduces *stereotype threat* with the following example. A White student sits in an African American studies class at Columbia University. All of the other students and the professor are Black. He wants to raise his hand and contribute to class, but every time he begins to raise his hand, he is overcome by anxiety and he cannot communicate a lucid idea. His brain is flooded with fearful thoughts that if he opens his mouth, he will confirm a stereotype about how White people are insensitive or racist. He is experiencing *stereotype threat.*

Students from any background can experience stereotype threat depending on the context. Students with disabilities, students of color, non-native English speakers, first-generation college students, or LGBTQ+ students may all experience stereotype threat in different contexts. Three conditions trigger stereotype threat. The first is when students are doing something they find challenging, performing at the threshold of their skills. The second is when they are in an environment where the majority of peers and authority figures are not from their ethnic/racial or cultural background or identity. The third is when they are engaging in an activity in which they are afraid of confirming a stereotype about the cultural group with which they identify.

Stereotype threat can be artificially triggered. In one study, both Black and White male students from Columbia were given a golf test. If the researchers told students that the test measured their intellectual capacity, the Black students exhibited signs of stereotype threat and performed poorly. If they told students that the test measured their physical agility, then the White students exhibited signs of stereotype threat and performed poorly. Something as small as a checked box on a test can trigger stereotype threat, as well. Black or female students did worse on a test if they were asked to check a box about their race or gender, because it triggered stereotype threat (Steele, 2010). Krendl, Richeson, Kelley, and Heatherton (2008) observed that women's performance on a difficult math test suffered after the treatment group was told the test previously had revealed gender differences in performance. Stereotype threat causes neurological and physiological symptoms. The functional magnetic resonance imaging (fMRI) results in the Krendl et al. study showed that for students experiencing stereotype threat there was increased activity in the ventral anterior cingulate cortex, the emotional regulation part of the brain. The fMRI showed that for students not experiencing stereotype threat there was increased activity in the prefrontal cortex, the area of the brain associated with solving math problems (see Figure 3.5). Osborne (2007) found that women experiencing stereotype threat did more poorly on a GRE-type test and had increased sweating, surface skin temperature, and diastolic blood pressure. Stereotype threat hijacks executive functioning, interferes with performance, and has negative physiological effects. The next section addresses what we can do to support students who are at risk for experiencing stereotype threat.

Four Everyday Moves That Alleviate Stereotype Threat

In this section, I discuss four research-based psychological interventions that I use every day while I teach classes with high percentages of students of color, immigrant students, non-native English speakers, formerly incarcerated students, first-generation college students, and students with disabilities.

Values Affirmation Exercises. The first move to alleviate stereotype threat is *values affirmation exercises.* In one study, a 20-minute values affirmation exercise improved academic outcomes for 7th-grade Black

Figure 3.5. Your Brain on Stereotype Threat

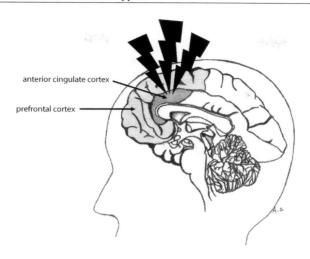

students (Cohen, Garcia, Apfel, & Master, 2006). In this double-blind randomized control study, the treatment group was asked to write down three core values and then write a paragraph about why those values were important to the students. This simple intervention reduced the Black–White achievement gap in these classes by 40%. White students in the treatment groups did not see a corresponding improvement in achievement. Think back to the drawing activity, Finding Your Growth Mindset. Part of the power of this growth mindset drawing activity lies in the fact that not only does it launch growth mindset, but it invites students to explore a passionate interest and therefore affirms their core values in a college setting. According to Cohen et al., "Self-affirmations, by buttressing self-worth, can alleviate the stress arising in threatening performance situations" (p. 1308). Self-affirmations also can help students enhance their feelings of belonging. What opportunities do you provide for students to affirm their core values in your course?

Three-Tiered Feedback. The second stereotype move is Claude Steele's *wise feedback* (Yeager et al., 2014). This is a *three-tiered feedback* move that alleviates stereotype threat and motivates students to excel (Cohen, Steele, & Ross, 1999). The three tiers are: (1) providing critical feedback; (2) holding the student to the same high standards as everyone else; and (3) communicating "I believe you can do it."

Critical feedback is the typical feedback that instructors write on essays or math problems to help students understand their mistakes and improve their skills. Critical feedback can be particularly threatening to students of color who fear that the instructor thinks that they do not belong in the college classroom. In one study, African American students were put into three groups. The first group received critical feedback and the message that they were being held to high standards. The second group received critical feedback with the message, "I believe in you." However, the third group received critical feedback *and* the message that they were held to high standards, *and* the message that the instructor believed in them. The third group performed the best. In this study, the instructor simply wrote, "I am giving you this feedback because I believe in you," on student papers. I gave an example of this three-tiered feedback in Chapter 2 at the end of Byron Reaves's story when an instructor spent 45 minutes giving him critical feedback on an assignment. Three examples of Steele's wise feedback are in Table 3.4.

Avoiding Comfort-Oriented Praise. The third move that alleviates stereotype threat is *avoiding comfort-oriented praise*. Although we want to communicate to our students that we care about them, comfort-oriented praise demotivates minority students. In one study, providing comfort-oriented praise undermined the success of ethnic/racial minority students in math (Rattan, Good, & Dweck, 2012). The study found that when instructors had a fixed mindset about student learning, they tended to comfort students whom they perceived as having low math ability. They implemented "kind" strategies like assigning less homework or calling on the student less. Students perceived the instructor as having lower expectations for them, and they lowered their own expectations for their performance correspondingly—and thus became demotivated. Examples of comfort-oriented praise from the study are: "I want to assure you that I know you are a talented student in general—it's just not the case that everyone is a 'math person,'" and "I want you to remember how great you do in other subjects."

Using probing questions and focusing on skill development can help instructors avoid the tendency to give comfort-oriented praise. Rather than not calling on students, to avoid causing them "added pressure," we can create a learning environment where students view mistakes and false paths as sources of learning; where students know that the issue is not that they are bad at a subject, but rather that they have not mastered

Table 3.4. Wise Feedback

	Example 1: Essay Draft with Written Feedback
Critical Feedback	This first draft of your essay demonstrated many strong writing skills. I have included comments on the attached rubric to identify skills in which you can continue to improve.
High Standards	All students in this course must improve their writing skills to meet the expectations of a transfer-level course.
"I believe in you"	Your past work has demonstrated that you have the adaptive skills and commitment to work hard, to incorporate my feedback, and to revise and continue to improve your writing skills. You are not there, YET. I believe you can build these skills.
	Example 2: Oral Presentation with One-on-One Oral Feedback
Critical Feedback	As stated in our one-on-one meeting, this is a strong first round of your persuasive presentation. Please check my notes and comments on your scored rubric for ideas on how to continue to improve your skills.
High Standards	The goal of this assignment is to create a presentation that showcases your communication skills in order to convince an audience of potential investors to invest in your product.
"I believe in you"	I know from examples in your work portfolio and contributions to class discussions that you will be able to implement my suggestions and improve the quality and persuasiveness of your presentation to meet the expectations for this assignment.
	Example 3: Chemistry Exam with Written Feedback
Critical Feedback	Please read my feedback and comments on your exam to assess which skills you need to continue to improve.
High Standards	In order to demonstrate a mastery of the topics and skills in this college-level chemistry course, students must invest adequate time and develop strategies that enable them to learn all the material covered in the text, lectures, and labs. In addition, students must be proficient at writing at the college level.
"I believe in you"	You have demonstrated strong study skills and strong conceptual understanding of many of the chemistry topics so far. For example, you take complete notes, have strong skills for converting units of measurement, and are precise with measuring in lab. If you continue to develop your study strategies; develop your essay-writing skills; and spend adequate time improving your understanding of the remaining topics, I know you will excel in this class.

Adapted from Interventioncentral.org.

a specific content-area skill, *yet*. We want students to embrace challenges and uncomfortable moments, so they have more opportunities to improve their skills. We want to communicate that we have the same expectations for all students.

Normalizing Apprehension. The fourth stereotype move is *normalizing apprehension*. One study found that Black college students tended to interpret adverse experiences in college as indications that they did not belong in the academic setting (Walton & Cohen, 2007). I notice this in my first-gen students, as well. The Walton and Cohen study found that Blacks, but not Whites, benefitted from a normalizing apprehension intervention, which nurtured social belonging to reduce stereotype threat. In this study, students were told two things: (1) having some tough days at college is normal, and all students, regardless of race, experience it when transitioning to college; and (2) these issues get better over time. I add a third growth mindset message when I use this intervention: (3) you will develop strategies over time that will help you get better at dealing with these tough times. I use this normalizing messaging almost every day with first-generation college students, students of color, and students with learning disabilities who communicate to me that they feel they don't belong in college. Still, it is important not to minimize or negate the experiences of discrimination that students of color, formerly incarcerated, bilingual, or other students experience when you are normalizing apprehension.

Recent research indicates that these stereotype threat interventions do not benefit just students at risk of experiencing stereotype threat, either. A meta-analysis of several studies indicated that *all* students in a class benefit when stereotype threat is alleviated for students experiencing it (Powers et al., 2016). To find out more and to get better at using stereotype threat interventions in your classroom, read Steele's *Whistling Vivaldi* (2010).

OTHER EQUITY MOVES

In this section I describe five other activities or strategies that promote equity.

First Impressions

One way to launch a class is with my activity, **First Impressions**. Instead of introducing myself on the first day of my education courses, I post 10–20 statements about myself like the ones that follow. Some of them are true; some are not. Students work in groups and discuss which are true and which are not. Then I walk through the list as a way to introduce myself and to launch a discussion about stereotype bias.

1. Instructor is monolingual in English.
2. Instructor is bilingual in Spanish and English.
3. One of the instructor's parents obtained a doctoral degree.
4. Neither of the instructor's parents attained a bachelor's degree.
5. In 1985, instructor worked as a farm laborer castrating pigs, milking cows, and mason-tending.
6. In 1985, instructor earned a Viticulture and Enology Certificate for distinguishing wines from different regions in France including Bourdeaux, Avignon, Dijon, and Normandy.
7. Instructor has a brother who was a commodities trader of Southeast Asian artifacts in the Upper East Side of Manhattan for 8 years specializing in Austronesian (Proto-Malay and Deutero-Malay) and Austroasiatic (Mon, Khmer, and Viet-Muong) groups.
8. Instructor has a brother who was incarcerated for a violent crime in upstate New York for 8 years.

(The truths are 2, 4, 5, 8.) Because the activity is framed in terms of identity and biases, and because I share so much about myself, it models for students how to do the second part of this opening activity. The second part is called **Assumptions and Surprises**. Students write four things about their identity: two true and two false. This is not the game "two truths and a lie," because students will share specific aspects of their core identities that may not be evident. Also, they play a little bit with societal biases and stereotypes because of my modeling. They are invited to share as much or as little as they want. I had a student who had fair skin, but was Mexican, write as the lie, "I am White." An Asian student wrote, "I am great at math," to play with the stereotype. Another student wrote, "The last time I hugged my father was 15 years ago." It was the truth. Students frequently write things that one could get wrong just by looking at the surface of their identities.

Mentoring

One of the most common questions I am asked in my role as professional development provider for educators is, "How can I mentor students who are from different class, ethnic, and cultural backgrounds than mine?" I tell instructors, "It is normal to feel apprehensive about mentoring students who are from different cultural backgrounds and identify differently than you. All instructors who are developing the skills of mentoring these students feel awkward at first. You will get better with time as you experiment, develop new strategies, and refine your skills." Notice here, that I used the normalizing apprehension technique mentioned earlier, with a little bit of growth mindset approach thrown in. Many White or middle-class instructors experience some anxiety when they reach out to students from class or ethnic/racial backgrounds different than their own. They worry, "What if I say something insensitive that can be construed as racist or classist?" Developing your own skills for moving past those fears is a natural part of the process.

My advice is just to treat people as people. Talk to them. Be curious. Ask about their family. Ask about their work. Ask about their dreams. Invite them to your office. If they are deaf or hard of hearing or have a visual impairment, ask them how they would like you to refer to their disability. Ask a lot of questions and make no assumptions. "Is it okay to say_____? Do you say visually impaired or blind? What do you prefer? How am I doing? Let me know if you would like any help with your wheelchair." However, their answers do not reflect what everybody thinks who has that disability or is from that ethnic/racial background. Of course, do not call them out in class as an example. For instance, if you are talking about sexual identity, do not say, "Let's hear from Ellen; she does not identify as cis female." I have mentored Latinx, African American, and Asian students from high school to doctoral programs, and I am White. I am better than I was before, but not as good as I am going to be.

If you are White and mentoring a student of color, communicate Steele's *three-tier wise feedback* or use the *normalizing apprehension intervention*. Give students opportunities to *affirm their core values* in conversations and in writing. Students of color navigate a different social structure than White students. They are wise to mistrust the system, because it has let them down in the past. Your anxiety over reaching out to them is not as important as your need to build trust with them. If you are reaching out to them because you believe that they can do it and you want to help them achieve their goals, they will feel that. I have a few African American students each semester. I make sure to connect with them early and give them lots of growth mindset feedback and growth mindset praise. I give the three-tiered wise feedback; I normalize apprehension; and I ask them questions that give them opportunities to affirm their values. I make them feel like they belong. I email or call them if they are absent. In these moments, I am disrupting the larger systemic inequity. Many students who historically have been discriminated against by larger systems assume that you are part of those systems. I commit to being one of the standout faculty members who disrupts the system for them at the classroom level. I am still learning too, and reading books, attending workshops, and joining social media groups that focus on race, sexual orientation, gender, disabilities, and language all help.

Assigning Competence in Groups

Assigning competence to "low-status" students is another equity move that communicates, "I believe in you" (Cohen & Lotan, 2004; Cohen, Lotan, Scarloss, & Arellano, 1999). If an instructor allots more air time to the White, monolingual, heterosexual, cisgender, affluent students than to students who historically feel like outsiders, students will notice it. Students who have been subjected to a system that is unfair probably will assume that this classroom is just like the outside world paradigm. That is why the whole idea of assigning competence is such a high-leverage equity move. This feedback/praise strategy lets students know that you value them, and it is a key part of Cohen and Lotan's (2004) *complex instruction*. Complex instruction involves students engaging in challenging, inquiry-based learning in groups. Also, complex instruction "aims to disrupt typical hierarchies of who is smart and who is not" (Sapon-Shevin, 2004, p 3). Basically, Cohen and Lotan advocate assigning competence to students in groups that society or other students in the class may regard as having lower status. This may mean non-native English speakers, students of color, or students with disabilities. However, groups are unique, and the "lower-status" student is not necessarily a student who is discriminated against in the larger society. For example, a student in a group may just speak more slowly than the others in that group, and you notice that the others frequently interrupt the student who speaks slowly.

Mary Ann was a tall, affluent, White female student in my pre-algebra class. She was quite aggressive to me, even a little condescending. She boasted about her family's substantial assets and her job at the Lamborghini dealership. I randomized groups every week. However, regardless of which group she was in, there were always students who were marginalized in her group. One day, I was circulating around the room as students solved problems related to subtracting negative numbers. I noticed Anahi's desk was very far away from the desks of the other two people in Mary Ann's group. Seeing that Anahi was not getting the benefit of working in a group, I crouched next to her desk and asked her to tell me a little about her approach to solving the problem. She explained it in a way that I had never heard before (in 30 years), so I asked her if I could share her novel approach with the entire class. I excitedly went to the board and had her coach me on what to write and say in order to explain her approach. In saying, "Anahi's approach is innovative and very strong conceptually," I assigned competence to the contribution of a lower-status student in the group. Not only did Anahi benefit from this equity move, but the whole class benefitted from hearing her original approach. On the next quiz, two other students used her approach to solving the problem. Assigning competence is an equity move that communicates, "I will make sure we hear from everyone in the room. In that spirit, I'm going to amplify, I'm going to ramp up what this one person said, here. I will communicate to this 'lower'-status student in the group that I notice and value what they are saying." This is also a way to verbally communicate, "I believe in you." Ultimately, when students hear diverse perspectives, it improves learning for everyone.

Videos

I am a White female from the northeastern United States, but most of my students are first-generation-college Latinx, African American, Native American, or Pacific Islander. Therefore, I supplement instruction with videos led by instructors of color. I showed one video of Dana W. Harris, owner of Young Guru Online Math Tutoring (@ygmathtutoring), in which he solved multi-step equations. He was completely different than me physically and culturally. He was African American and male, had a very long beard and a closely shaved head, wore a T-shirt, and spoke a southern U.S. dialect. I told my students, "Dana and I are of the same mind. We are cut from the same cloth. We both emphasize teaching concepts over rules. We both encourage students to take their own unique approach to solving equations, and not just to follow some algorithmic approach." Also, I pointed out some things that I learned from him. In this way, I did not simply show a video of an African American man teaching math, but I highlighted the expertise of an authority figure that looked more like my students than I do.

Social Justice Activities

While it is important to reach out and mentor students of color, you may be drawn to connect your course content to messages around social justice. For example, if you teach U.S. history, maybe you connect the U.S. internment of Japanese people during World War II with current events in 2019, when the U.S. government is separating children from their parents and housing them in detainment facilities. Below is an example of a social justice math problem that Dan Munton, a community college math instructor, created and taught for a statistics unit. Dan downloaded Department of Justice data. He constructed contingency tables (one is shown below) and had students analyze them to see whether there was enough evidence to conclude that Ferguson police were racially profiling African American residents. Students learned about statistics while they engaged in a social justice activity. The complete activity can be found at feliciadarling.com. The directions for the problem are as follows:

> You are a statistical consultant, hired to determine if the tables provide evidence of racial profiling or discrimination. You will accomplish this by computing two conditional probabilities for each table (and other probabilities, if desired) and explaining what the probabilities mean and how they do or do not provide evidence of racial profiling. Identify the events by letters and use proper notation throughout.

Contingency Table

	Arrested	Not Arrested	Total Stopped
African American	483	4,149	4,632
Caucasian	36	650	686
Total	519	4,799	5,318

Some other social justice resources are: Howard Zinn's *A People's History of the United States*; Jonathan Osler's *A Guide for Integrating Issues of Social and Economic Justice into Mathematics Curriculum*; the Science and Social Justice Project at Harvard; Teaching Social Justice in the Physics Classroom at Kalamazoo College; and www.kzoo.edu/praxis/.

This chapter addressed the topic of instructor and student mindsets that bolster success for all students. It invites instructors to examine their implicit biases and to approach fostering a growth mindset using an equity lens. In addition, it discussed stereotype threat to help instructors become better mentors of students with stories radically different than their own. In Chapter 4, we will discuss educational psychology theory essential for teaching the model of inquiry-based group learning that is illustrated in Chapter 5.

Ed Psych Theory 2.0

> Becoming informed about education theory is how we stand on the shoulders of education experts who came before us to improve our own instruction.

Many U.S. community college instructors have not taken an education psychology (ed psych) course for 10 to 20 years. Others have never taken an ed psych course at all. This chapter is an opportunity for instructors to become familiar with or to refamiliarize themselves with foundational ed psych theory and how it can inform their instruction. These theories are pivotal for developing instruction that emphasizes the active, inquiry-based and group learning that is described in Chapter 5. Also, exploring the connection between ed psych theory and the high-impact classroom practices we use every day can be both confirming and inspiring.

Behaviorism, constructivism, socioculturalism, and social constructivism are four foundational theories that are key for responding to the learning approaches of 21st-century community college students. Other key theories discussed in this chapter include Vygotsky's zone of proximal development, Sweller's cognitive load theory, Piaget's theory of cognitive disequilibrium and prior knowledge, and Bloom's taxonomy for promoting higher-order thinking.

FOUR APPROACHES TO LEARNING AND TEACHING

The four foundational educational theories discussed in this section have important implications for teaching and learning. An understanding of these approaches helps to illustrate why asset-based instruction, inquiry-based group learning, and fostering positive academic mindsets framed with an equity lens are best practices for 21st-century college classrooms.

Behaviorism: Teaching Is Telling

Back when some of us went to school, in the last half of the 20th century, educators subscribed to a more behaviorist approach to education. In behaviorist theory, students are regarded as empty vessels, and teachers are the authorities in the room that fill their empty heads with objective knowledge (Figure 4.1). In behaviorist classrooms, students sit in straight rows, and the instructor focuses primarily on the lecture style of instruction, known as direct instruction. In the behaviorist model, instructors are the authorities on a subject who transmit objective knowledge to students. Students are rewarded for repeating back to the instructors the knowledge that was transmitted to them.

Behaviorism operates on the principle of stimulus and response. "I say, you do." Students get points for doing what the teacher says, as teaching and learning involve a system of rewards for correct performance and behavior. Also, student behavior is interpreted without any consideration for the internal process, as prior knowledge is largely ignored. Learning is regarded as filling an empty vessel (students' brains) with objective knowledge. It is reminiscent of Freire's (2000) banking model of education, where instructors make "deposits" in students.

It is common for many of us instructors to begin our teaching profession with a bent toward a behaviorist approach, because we were taught like that. Amy Flores Roscielle, Math and College Skills instructor, explains what it was like when she began teaching math 15 years ago: "It took me 2 years to even realize that the way I taught math was based on the way that I had learned math in elementary and high school. Then, it took another 3 years to learn how to integrate teaching to include [instruction], beyond just focusing on content knowledge." She worked on developing instructional strategies, curriculum, assessment, and student work analysis by engaging in faculty communities of practice, professional development, and reading groups. In sum, behaviorism—while it has its role in instruction—is not the current gold standard for teaching 21st-century community college students.

Constructivism: Students Construct Knowledge

Based on emerging neuroscience and cognition research, K–16 education is shifting away from the behaviorist approach. Education leaders advocate more constructivist (Piaget, 1952) and socioculturalist (Vygotsky, 1978) approaches. You already may be teaching with both a constructiv-

Figure 4.1. Behaviorist Theory of Education

ist and a socioculturalist approach when you use group-work, facilitate classroom discussions, tap into students' prior knowledge, ask probing questions, assign projects, and provide varied assessments.

Constructivism is a theory that views learning as a complex process in which learners construct knowledge by drawing from and building upon their past experiences and prior knowledge. In constructivism, teachers facilitate learning with students by connecting students' prior knowledge to the current learning goals. As an example, a chemistry instructor wants students to learn the concept of phase transition, specifically the idea of whether substances require energy to change to a solid, liquid, or gas state. Students are unfamiliar with these concepts. First, she reviews the idea that heat is energy. All students have prior experience with hot and cold water, but may not have experience with other substances like selenium, titanium, and helium. Therefore, the instructor launches the lesson by asking questions about water—in its liquid form, solid form (ice), and gaseous form (steam)—in order to tap into students' prior knowledge. She asks students, "If you want to change ice, a solid, into a liquid, would you cool it or heat it? If you want to turn a quart of water into a gas, would you cool it or heat it?" Then she makes the point that all substances act in the same manner as water. This is an example of helping

Table 4.1. Differences Between Constructivism and Behaviorism

Constructivism	Behaviorism
Believes learning is constructed knowledge; students possess a wealth of prior knowledge and experiences	Believes learning is transmitted knowledge; students are empty vessels to be filled with knowledge
Views educators as facilitators who encourage students to explore within a constructed framework	Views educators as objective authorities who primarily use lecture and direct instruction to tell/teach
Emphasizes the learning process and values incremental growth, mistakes, false paths, and revisions (growth mindset)	Emphasizes a system that provides rewards and reinforcements for correct answers and performance (fixed mindset)
Explicitly connects course content to students' prior knowledge and backgrounds	Regards course content as objective and unrelated to students' knowledge and backgrounds
Illuminates the unique perspectives and approaches of students	Illuminates only instructors' knowledge/perspective of the content
Focuses on deepening conceptual understanding and procedural (factual) knowledge	Focuses more on procedural (factual) knowledge than on conceptual understanding

students to construct knowledge about a new chemistry topic by building on their prior knowledge. Starting from the common recognition of water in three states, students can move more easily to understanding that all materials have their own specific temperatures at which they transition from liquid to solid to gas.

With a constructivist approach, instructors scaffold learning and facilitate a student's construction of knowledge. Research indicates that a constructivist approach improves learning. Some key differences between constructivism and behaviorism are listed in Table 4.1.

Socioculturalism: Students Are Teachers, Too

A socioculturalist (Vygotsky, 1978) instructional approach interfaces kindly with the constructivist approach. Socioculturalism asserts that social interaction plays a fundamental role in the development of cognition; learning is social. In addition, it asserts that prior knowledge is not just prior content knowledge, but the sum of all of a student's real-life home and cultural experiences. An example of a sociocultural approach in a classroom is when a teacher asks students to work in groups to create a poster describing how they made sense out of and solved a physics word problem or when a class of recent immigrants reads a book like, *On Becoming Dr. Q*, about an immigrant who became a doctor. Furthermore, socioculturalism embraces the idea that content knowledge is learned not just in schools, but that students bring with them a wealth of funds of knowledge, a term invented by Louis Moll (Moll, Amanti, Neff, & Gonzalez, 1992), from families and communities. This knowledge is not necessarily taught in school but is relevant to the subject area.

The following is an example from my study conducted in a Yucatec Maya village where local community members use cultural assets of autonomy and improvisation to solve math problems in everyday life. Motorcycle taxi drivers there calculate their mileage in innovative ways without gas gauges or odometers. They use fares collected, time driving, and centimeters of gas in their gas tank as proxies to calculate mileage. Students bring this wealth of specialized community math expertise to middle school math classrooms where it is sometimes overlooked (Darling, 2017, 2019). Socioculturalism recognizes students' funds of knowledge, as well as the social nature of learning emphasized by neuroeducational theory.

Social Constructivism: Students Co-construct Knowledge with Peers

Social constructivism is a synthesis of socioculturalism and constructivism. Social constructivist theory does not assert simply that individual students construct knowledge by drawing from their own prior knowledge, as constructivism does. Social constructivism states that students co-construct knowledge together through social interaction with their peers and the instructor. While constructivism asserts that individual students construct knowledge, and teachers are facilitators in that process, social constructivism asserts that students co-construct knowledge through social interactions with their peers, and teachers facilitate these social interactions in order to scaffold learning (Figure 4.2).

This sociocultural constructivist approach is embodied in Jo Boaler's *Mathematical Mindset* (2016). In classrooms in Boaler's studies, students typically solve challenging, open-ended problems in groups. They are encouraged to experiment by taking risks and making mistakes. Students lean in and embrace and discuss one another's unique approaches to solving math problems. In groups, they explain and justify their reasoning. Instructors facilitate learning by asking probing or open-ended questions. Frequently, a social constructivist approach embraces real-life applications

Figure 4.2. Social Constructivist Theory of Education

as well. In Chapter 5, I illustrate what a social constructivist approach looks like in both an English and a math classroom where inquiry-based group learning is emphasized. However, in the balance of this chapter, we will examine other ed psych theories that are foundational to teaching today's community college students.

FIVE KEY THEORIES FOR 21st-CENTURY LEARNING AND TEACHING

Knowledge of the five enduring educational psychology theories in this section are key for teaching in today's college classrooms. While they have been informing instruction in kindergarten through 12th-grade classrooms for decades, frequently instructors at the college level have not had the opportunity to formally explore them. For those readers who have already been exposed to them, revisiting them can be illuminating.

Zone of Proximal Development

Another concept key for inquiry-based learning is Vygotsky's concept of the *zone of proximal development* (Berk & Winsler, 1995). The zone of proximal development (ZPD) is the gap between where students' independent skills are right now in terms of their mastery of the content and where their independent skills will be after their learning has been supported with facilitating and "scaffolding" provided by an instructor (Vygotsky, 1978). Scaffolding refers to a variety of instructional techniques that instructors implement to stair-step students toward independent mastery of learning. Two examples are when an instructor: (1) models paired conversations before students work in pairs; and (2) asks students to write their ideas down before they share them orally in groups.

In Vygotsky's model, there are three zones of learning. The first is the *zone of actual development* (ZAD), a student's comfort zone, where a student can already perform a task independently, without the support of an instructor. We do not want to teach in a student's comfort zone. If students have mastered the content already, they will be too comfortable, bored, and unengaged with the learning process. The next zone of learning is the *zone of proximal development*. This is the key zone to pay attention to in order to maximize the potential for learning. This is the zone of learning where a student can accomplish a task or skill with expert scaffolding and facilitation from the instructor. This is the student's reach zone, where a student can achieve the learning targets of the day when provided with specific supports. Students are engaged and motivated when learning in their reach zone. The third zone is called the *zone of eventual development* (ZED), where a student cannot grasp the concepts yet—even with expert facilitation and support from the instructor. This is a student's anxiety zone. We do not want to teach in a student's anxiety zone. If we teach students in their ZED, no matter what support we provide, the mastery of desired skills and knowledge is out of the students' reach, and they will feel defeated, detached, or agitated. See Figure 4.3, which builds upon Senninger's (2000) learning zone model.

Let's look at a specific example in a Spanish class (Figure 4.4). Martin arrives at class on Tuesday with two skills he can perform independently. First, he can use the present tense in Spanish conversations. Second, he can describe, in English, countries he likes to or does not like to visit. These two skills are in Martin's *comfort zone* (ZAD). The learning target for Tuesday's class is for students to be able to discuss in Spanish, in pairs, the countries that they like or countries they think they might like to visit and why.

This learning target is in Martin's *reach zone*, his ZPD. The instructor scaffolds the lesson by having students think about which countries they have visited and which ones they liked and did not like. Then students

Figure 4.3. Emotions in Three Different Zones of Learning

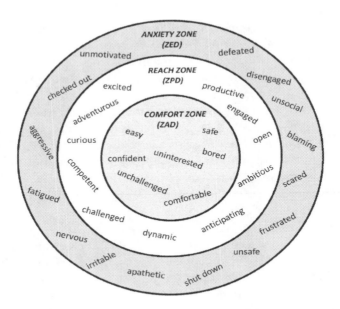

write in Spanish about what they like and do not like about countries they visited. Then she provides each student pair with sentence starters and frames on index cards in Spanish to begin their discussions. Students take turns asking the questions on the cards and using the sentence starters. Students already had practiced in previous classes how to have discussions in pairs. This is an example of how a teacher scaffolds learning for students in their ZPD or reach zone. Skills that students have in their ZPD become skills they have in their ZAD.

What about the fact that students have different reach zones, because they come to class with different skills? What about Kayla, the student from a lower-income household who has never visited another country? Or Anahi, who has not mastered the skills of using Spanish in the present tense? What about Parnell, who has not mastered the basics of doing academic discussion in pairs? Or Petra, who already mastered the learning target for Tuesday's class? How do we teach students who arrive in class with different gaps in knowledge and skills, who come from different cultural and class backgrounds? The remaining chapters in the book address these instructional challenges.

Figure 4.4. Learning in the Three Zones in Spanish Class

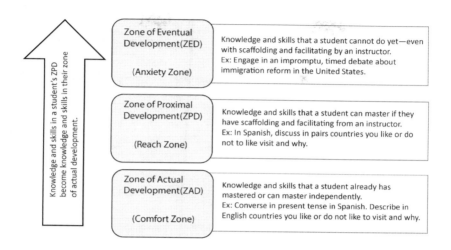

To get a better idea of what students experience in different zones, take a few moments to think about which learning zone you are in when learning how to do the tasks in Table 4.2.

The following is an example of a student who was learning outside of her ZPD in pre-algebra class. Marla Carrington was a radiation technician. At age 58 she returned to community college to get her nursing degree. She attended class every day, worked hard on her homework, went to the tutorial lab, but was getting Ds and Fs on quizzes and tests. On Day 16 of class, Marla had tears in her eyes and looked overwhelmed. She was learning outside her zone of proximal development. She came to my office and said, "I am struggling. I have a tutor and spend over 20 hours a week in the tutorial lab. Still, I always feel behind and get nothing from class lectures, because I never know what is going on." I said, "Many students in your class have taken a class like this recently in high school, as they are only 18 or 20. It is largely review for them. However, you have come to class with very little recent prior knowledge of the material. You said that you never took algebra in high school." I gave her videos to watch before class, so she could she pre-learn the **materials** before class. In this way she could learn in her reach zone during class instead of in her anxiety zone. In this situation, I used growth mindset strategies (focused on skills instead of ability), stereotype threat strategies (normalizing ap-

Table 4.2. What Zone Are You in?

Learning Task	Comfort Zone	Reach Zone	Anxiety Zone
Communicating directions using ASL to a person who is deaf			
Preparing a gourmet dinner for 20			
Solving a physics problem on thermodynamics			
Communicating your life story in French			
Using CPR to rescue a drowning victim			
Balancing your checkbook			
Facilitating a discussion about ethnic/racial discrimination			

prehension), and a simple scaffolding strategy of pre-learning the material using a video.

Marla watched a video on scientific notation before next class. When I asked the class, "What do you remember about scientific notation?" to tap into prior knowledge, Marla confidently talked about how to move the decimals; why scientific notation was useful in rewriting really big or small numbers; and why she preferred one method over the other. She was able to access the instruction because she was actually learning in her zone of proximal development, and she was able to connect her prior knowledge to the day's learning targets. By the 22nd class she told me, "I do not feel behind anymore." I joked with her that one day she would raise her hand and say, "This class is boring; you are going too slow." Her final test average was 96%.

In conclusion, students are comfortable or bored if you teach in their zone of actual development (comfort zone). They are engaged and motivated if you teach in their zone of proximal development (reach zone), but anxious or disengaged if you teach in their zone of eventual development (anxiety zone). The key to effective instruction is to provide facilitation and scaffolding to students in their ZPD—or reach zone. In Chapter 5, I describe inquiry-based learning and collaborative-learning strategies that address the needs of students with different ZPDs, or reach zones.

Cognitive Load Theory

A discussion of Sweller's (2011) cognitive load theory also must include a discussion of Piaget's (1952) theory of cognitive disequilibrium and activating students' prior knowledge.

The two important assumptions of Sweller's cognitive load theory (Sweller et al., 2011) are: (1) meaning is personally constructed by the learner and is influenced by prior knowledge, experiences, and beliefs; and (2) students are more likely to store information into long-term memory if cognitive load is reduced and the material is connected to their prior knowledge (Sweller, Ayres, & Kalyuga, 2011). Working memory is the system for storing or managing information needed for accomplishing cognitively demanding tasks. Long-term memory is the retention of knowledge and skills for an extended period of time. In order to help learners leverage their working memory to maximize the potential for information to be stored in their long-term memory, we must design instruction with the three types of cognitive load in mind. They are intrinsic load, extraneous cognitive load, and germane load.

Intrinsic Load. *Intrinsic load* is inherent in a task and cannot be lessened by the instructor. For example, completing this task: 2 + 2 = ? has a smaller intrinsic load than completing this task: .3356789 + .432001 = ? Some tasks are intrinsically more challenging than others. If you are teaching an anatomy course, there is a certain amount of information that needs to be processed because it is integral to the course. An instructor cannot water down curriculum. However, one can notify students ahead of time if a particular skill might be challenging, in order to normalize their apprehension about its difficulty.

Extraneous Cognitive Load. Unlike intrinsic load, *extraneous cognitive load* is completely managed by the method in which an instructor chooses to facilitate learning. For example, an instructor who wanted to teach the anatomy of a frog, could (1) tell students to silent-read 30 pages in the text about the anatomy of a frog; (2) show an instructional video on the anatomy of a frog; or (3) take students into the lab where they worked in groups on structured activities to dissect, identify, and discuss the parts of a frog. The first method has more extraneous load, because it provides students with 30 pages of text they must decipher independently in order to access content. In general, we want to reduce extraneous load for students. Graphic organizers are one way to do that. The two diagrams in Figure 4.5 use **graphic organizers** to illustrate the bones in the foot. It is clear that the diagram on the top minimizes extraneous load. The juxtaposition of random symbols, fonts, information, and patterns in the diagram on the bottom adds extra cognitive load for students trying to learn the bones of the foot. Perhaps an instructor could communicate the bones of the foot with the top diagram and then include the additional information in the bottom diagram in a paragraph or in table form. Strategically using fonts, patterns, or symbols can help organize written information for students so they can process new knowledge more effectively.

Germane Load. The third type of load, *germane load*, describes the cognitive load that is germane to students' lived experiences. Instructors have a lot of control over maximizing the germane load—the load that is relevant to students' prior knowledge and backgrounds. Maximizing germane load leads to changes in a student's knowledge and schema. As with instructors, students come to class with existing schemas that evolve over time from interactions with new knowledge. Examples of scaffolding strategies that capitalize upon students' germane load are hands-on activities, open-ended tasks, flowcharts, **concept maps,** collaborative learning, asking **high press questions,** and **chunking** (Marzano, 2007). The following is an example of reorganizing a task to maximize the germane load by using chunking.

Look at the following row of 15 letters for 30 seconds: BUAIMTF-CISCABAA. Cover them and then try to memorize them. How did you do? Was this hard or easy? Now, look at the following row of 15 letters for 30 seconds: ABCFBIUSACIAATM. Cover them and then try to memorize them. How did you do? Was this easier?

We recognize ABC, FBI, USA, CIA, and ATM because they are germane to our lived experiences in the United States. This reorganizing of the letters taps into our prior knowledge. We chunk information into *meaningful* patterns to move it from sensory memory to working memory—and sometimes into long-term memory—if it is made germane to our lives. Chunking and making material relevant to students' lives are two moves to help students store material into their long-term memory.

Piaget's Cognitive Disequilibrium

Like instructors, students possess existing schemas about the world and everything in it based on their prior experiences and learning. A schema is a mental or cognitive architecture that people develop to adapt to

Figure 4.5. Minimizing Extraneous Load

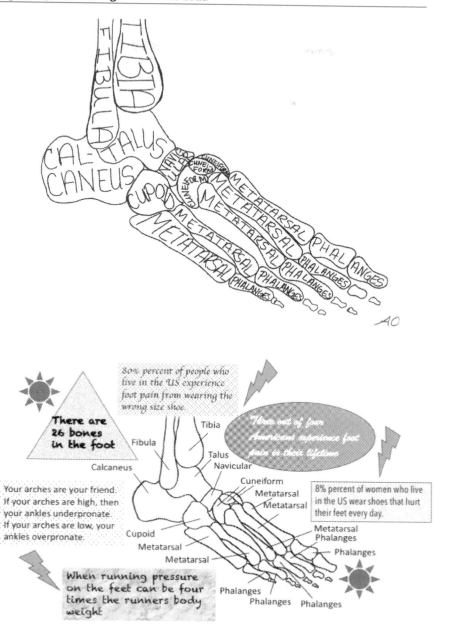

and organize their world. Instructors' schemas were discussed in Chapter 1. When students' individual schemas conflict with new knowledge they acquire, they experience *cognitive dissonance or disequilibrium*. This is a desirable moment in the learning process that educators refer to as a "teachable moment."

According to Piaget, a learner takes one of two approaches to reconcile the new knowledge with the existing schema. Learners either assimilate the new information or accommodate the new information. *Assimilation* means that the person incorporates this information into the existing schema with very little change to the existing schema. In the second case, a person *accommodates* the new knowledge by revising the existing schema.

An example of assimilation is when students are familiar with Microsoft Word and its range of functions, including spellcheck, word count, track changes, and so on. When they are introduced to a completely new word processing program, they can master it effortlessly by building on their existing schema about word processing programs. In an example of accommodation from a college biology class, students possess a schema that organs are located *inside* our bodies and perform a range of functions. Also, students have a schema that says skin is an inert sheath of material that protects the outside of the body. When the biology professor tells the students that skin is the largest organ of the body, they experience disequilibrium. When they accommodate this new information, they adapt their existing schema and say, "Oh, I guess organs *can* be outside the body and I guess skin performs more functions than just acting as a protective sheath."

Cognitive disequilibrium is a pivotal moment in learning, unlike cognitive overload. Cognitive overload causes students to shut down, similar to learning in their anxiety zone. While disequilibrium also may cause anxiety temporarily, still there is increased activity in many parts of the brain associated with learning. The following is an example of cognitive disequilibrium from one of my math classes. In an earlier class, we had discussed how $-3^2 \neq (-3)^2$. This is true, because $-3^2 = -1 \bullet (3) \bullet (3) = -9$. Also, we talked about how $(-3)^2 = (-3) \bullet (-3) = 9$. Finally, $-9 \neq 9$. This can be a difficult concept for pre-algebra students to really internalize. However, many students appeared to understand and accept it at the time. Later, I introduced a second example: $-(-3)^2 = -9$. One student, Nicole, said, "but last class you said that it equaled positive 9, because a negative times a negative equals a positive." She was having a difficult time accommodating this new knowledge as it seemed to conflict with a schema that she had adopted about the examples from the earlier class. I facilitated a discussion between several groups about this seeming contradiction. This was a moment of reconciling cognitive disequilibrium for some students. I said, "If this bothers you, then this is a powerful moment for you. You are engaged in this argument, and this is a great opportunity to learn. When you resolve this, you will be ahead of many math students and you will probably never be confused about this point again."

Activating Prior Knowledge

Many instructors activate students' prior knowledge when they are teaching a class. They may have a warm-up **math problem,** have students do a quick-write, or have them answer **launch prompts.** For example, an instructor can launch a discussion about conflict in literature by asking students to discuss their own experiences with internal conflicts, conflicts with nature, or conflicts with another person. It is powerful when an instructor explains why they do these tapping into-prior-knowledge activities in terms of neuroscience, as well. They can tell students that neural networks already exist in their brains around conflict. By tapping into prior knowledge, students are building on these existing neural networks to create new neural connections that will help them store today's content in their long-term memory.

According to Piaget, these pre-activities activate prior knowledge about content and open doors to help students gain access to the content. However, from a sociocultural point of view, the definition of prior knowledge is expanded beyond student content knowledge about biology, math, history, or writing class. It also includes knowledge from students' home and community experiences and the sum of their knowledge about content, linguistic experiences, cultural identities, college and career skills, and learning approaches. The following task underscores the importance of developing classroom activities that tap into students' unique prior knowledge, because students' background knowledge and experiences are diverse.

Working individually, please put these nine pictures into groups of three that make sense to you (Figure 4.6). Many people from Western cultures will sort these pictures into a taxonomy such as the one in Figure 4.7. They put the three vegetables together, the three animals together, and the three tools together.

However, in a 1989 study by Rogoff and Morelli, the Kpelle people in Africa were asked to sort 20 similar objects into groups of three.

Figure 4.6. Categorize into Groups of Three

Figure 4.7. Groups of Three

CHAPTER 5

21st-Century Learning
Active, Inquiry-Based, Collaborative

> Good instruction provides the container in which students can freely ex-
> plore, experiment, improvise, take risks, make mistakes, and co-construct
> new knowledge. That is the sweet spot to create; structure that fosters
> freedom.

Well-designed inquiry-based learning uses high-impact, interactive tasks, productive conversations, and group-work to help students co-construct new knowledge. Some terms that describe this type of social construc-tivist learning are: active learning, inquiry-based learning, complex in-struction, collaborative learning, or project-based learning. The inqui-ry approach addresses the variety of gaps in content knowledge and college skills that students in community college and open-access col-lege frequently have. In addition, it is an inclusive approach as it elicits the unique perspectives of students from all backgrounds. This approach is correlated with improved student outcomes in an introductory col-lege biology course of 250 students (Walker, Cotner, Baepler, & Decker, 2008) and in high school and college math classes (Boaler, 2002; Cohen, Lotan, Scarloss, & Arellano, 1999).

Many instructors ask, "How can I redress the range in gaps in con-tent knowledge of students? How can I motivate and engage all students? How can I tap into students' prior knowledge? How can I do active learning without the class devolving into chaos?" The five sections in this chapter answer these questions. The first section illustrates examples of inquiry-based, active, group learning in English and math. The second discusses the neuroscience research that underscores why this instruction-al approach is so powerful. The third section describes launch activities that community college instructors can use on the first day of class. The fourth outlines guiding principles and practices that prepare instructors to implement this approach. Finally, the fifth section offers high-impact strategies for building a community of learners.

TWO EXAMPLES: ONE IN ENGLISH, ONE IN MATH

The Example in English

This example, created and facilitated by English instructor Ann Foster, is a series of inquiry-based collaborative activities with open-ended questions that constitutes a 4-week unit. She uses the activities to scaffold the learning of writing essays. She draws from the Reading Apprenticeship Program from WestEd in this particular series of activities.

Ann said the first iteration of this series of activities emerged from the need to teach students to read and summarize college-level essays. However, the final iteration involved having students build their skills of analyzing the structure of an essay in order to develop autonomy and agency around writing their own essays. This 4-week unit is knee-deep in skill building and develops three skills in a stair-step fashion. First, it teaches students the prerequisite skills of breaking down an essay into chunks. Second, it uses those skills as a springboard to teach students how to analyze the structure of any essay. Third, it teaches students to write powerful essays.

Before we break down Ann's series of activities, I would like to talk about the power of Ann's word choices. You may remember the term *chunking* from Chapter 4 (e.g., FBI, CIA, ABC). It describes the strategy of organizing information into manageable chunks that are more germane to a student's prior experience. This is a great strategy for improving long-term memory storage of new material. When teaching this unit, Ann capitalizes on research that found that chunking improved reading comprehension. However, because in the students' vernacular, "to chunk" means "to vomit," Ann tunes into students' lived experiences and substitutes the word *clustering* for "chunking." In addition, Ann introduces the word *architecture* in her activities to describe the "structure" of the essay. Language is powerful. The structure of an essay sounds like a static quality; like a cage. Structure implies that an essay exists without the writer. Ann's choice of the word *architecture* implies that the writer is a creator, an architect, of the essay. This shift in language likely taps into student agency more effectively. This is consistent with my own research, which suggests that students from Yucatec Maya communities soar when invited to tap into their autonomy.

To begin teaching the unit, Ann helps students understand that a paragraph operates as a unit of meaning, and that sometimes a paragraph performs as part of a larger cluster of paragraphs. She begins this series of activities by having students analyze the architecture of a short essay with only eight paragraphs. Each paragraph of this starter essay is numbered. She reads the essay with the class out loud. Then she models how to talk about the clusters by doing a think-aloud. She begins, "I know as a strategic reader that one of the things that helps me to summarize an essay is to look at clusters of meaning." She continues: "The first three paragraphs of this essay are all about the students and teacher in the classroom. It is a personal narrative. In the next two paragraphs, the author widens the lens and begins talking about Utah and not just about what happens in the classroom. In paragraph six . . . I am not sure yet what it represents." **Modeling** and **think-alouds** are great scaffolding strategies for facilitating inquiry-based learning in groups. They prevent groupwork from devolving into chaos.

Ann explicitly teaches that there are six or seven things that she is looking for as a reader and these define clusters. These patterns of organization (also called rhetorical strategies) are threshold concepts. Some of these are: a change in the point of view; a change in the topic; a shift in the tone from formal to informal; a shift in the pattern of organization. It takes Ann four or five classes to teach reading rhetorically, and it is used as a springboard for improving students' writing. Reading rhetorically involves writing actions such as comparing, contrasting, analyzing, and arguing. Notice that these words are at the top of Bloom's taxonomy of actions that promote higher-order thinking.

As she teaches reading rhetorically, she teaches descriptive outlining. This requires a student to write what is happening and then summarize it. Ann provides a gradual-release model for students. She begins with modeling a think-aloud with the short, eight-line essay. Then students use this clustering tool to analyze the architecture of an essay independently. Next they get into groups and justify how they chose to cluster the essay. Finally, each group writes a descriptive outline of the essay and then the class shares out and has a conversation about any variations between groups. They discuss these variations, and students "negotiate" and "justify" their choices, which are both moves that promote higher-order thinking. Students do this on a variety of types of essays, including personal narrative, comparison, and cause and effect. Ultimately, this process of clustering, analyzing the architecture of an essay, and writing a descriptive outline of an essay informs students' own writing processes. In the end, students learn how to write more powerful essays from this process. Also, a classic writing strategy is to reverse-outline one's own essay to revise it. Students now have this skill under their belt as well.

Ann could have taken a more direct-instruction, behaviorist approach to teaching essay writing. She could have asserted herself as the authority in the room, the bearer of objective knowledge. She simply could have lectured and dictated the proper structure of an essay. Then she could have provided feedback about how well students did or did not emulate her prescribed model. That is how many of us were taught to write essays. I had to unlearn that approach in order to become an effective writer in graduate school. Ann does "clustering" and group-work, because they capitalize on what students already know and do. We can see that Ann Foster's approach helps students have more autonomy because she shifts the focus away from writing the prescriptive five-paragraph essay toward building on students' own expertise. Her approach to teaching writing is deeply conceptual and gives students license to be creative. But how can she tell whether her social constructivist approach is working? To determine the effectiveness of her approach, Ann engages in the cycle of instruction improvement described in Chapter 1. She triangulates data about student learning to draw conclusions about the effectiveness of her approach—and then refines her approach accordingly.

In order to assess whether her approach is working, Ann examines several data points. First, students write both pre- and post-course essays. Four instructors work in teams to score these essays using rubrics. Instructors calibrate their scoring techniques by using a test essay, and then they grade student essays from all classes in teams. Students are graded on the higher of the two classroom essays. Ann noticed that after she began implementing this clustering activity, students performed a lot better on the second essay. In fact, 21 out of 22 students scored higher on the second essay after the implementation of this 4-week unit.

In addition to the calibrated scoring of the pre- and post-clustering-activity essays, Ann gives a pre- and post-course survey in the class to assess how well students are doing. In both surveys, she gives students the same essay to read and asks them two questions: (1) Was it hard to read this essay? and (2) What is the main theme of this essay? In the pre-survey, students say that the essay is easy, and in the post-survey, they say that the essay is hard. She speculates that in the post-survey, they realize the complexity of the essay after developing more analytical skills to decipher its architecture. As a final way to collect data to inform the refining of her instruction, Ann takes notes during the break and after class about how well the class went. She listens to students' comments and questions in class and uses this information to refine how she will deliver instruction in the next class. She says that her notes tell her that she needs to teach this clustering activity much earlier.

The Example in Math

In Jo Boaler's (2016) social constructivist approach, students solve complex math problems in groups and communicate their reasoning using visual representations. This approach both addresses the range of skill and knowledge gaps in classrooms and elicits the unique perspectives of students from diverse backgrounds. Messages about fostering positive student mindsets are woven throughout Jo's instructional model. However, in the following example, we focus on the inquiry-based and group-learning aspects of her model.

In Jo's classes, students work in small groups to solve low-floor/high-ceiling, open-ended problems with multiple entry points and solutions. A low-floor/high-ceiling task with multiple entry points means that students with a wide range of prior content knowledge and skills can access the task. "Low floor" means that students with fewer entry-level skills can access the content. "High ceiling" means that students with greater entry-level skills can push beyond their previous limits. "Multiple entry points" means that students can begin the problem from many different starting points, because the problem does not emphasize prescriptive algorithmic approaches or procedural knowledge. Jo's approach ensures that students with a range of skills can work within their reach zones (ZPDs).

The following example from Jo's workshop demonstrates the difference between an open-ended and closed task. An instructor could teach the algorithm that area of a rectangle equals length times width ($A = L \bullet W$) and then give students a worksheet with 20 problems and ask them to work independently to "calculate the area of these 20 rectangles." That is a closed task that has one correct solution and one correct algorithmic approach to each problem. That is not a good task for inquiry-based, group learning. Conversely, an instructor could give students a more open-ended, low-floor/high-ceiling task by having them work in groups to answer, "How many different ways can you make a rectangle with a 24 cm^2 area?" This is a better task. Figure 5.1 shows how one group of students came up with seven rectangles. In the latter example, a student who has less procedural and conceptual knowledge about area can begin thinking and talking about what area is, and maybe come up with one rectangle to begin with (the low-floor aspect of the task). A student who possesses strong procedural understanding (i.e., can calculate area of a rectangle easily) would be challenged to think about area more conceptually, thus deepening the individual's conceptual knowledge of area (the high-ceiling aspect of the task). Groups generate a range of solutions and approaches

Figure 5.1. Open-Ended Task

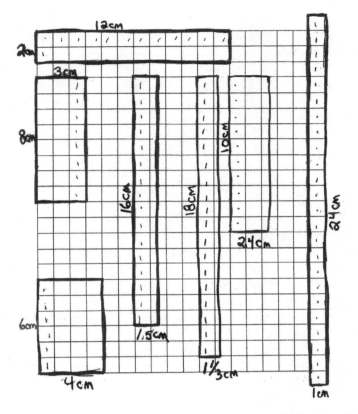

(multiple entry points). The instructor facilitates a whole-class discussion about assumptions inherent in students' approaches. Some students assume that they can use fractions or decimals. Others assume that if they use a rectangle that is 4 cm by 6 cm, then they cannot use a rectangle that is 6 cm by 4 cm. A group finds eight rectangles, if students assume that lengths have to be whole numbers and a 4 cm by 6 cm rectangle and a 6 cm by 4 cm rectangle are not unique rectangles. Another group finds an infinite number of rectangles, if students assume decimals and fractions can be used. This open-ended task has more entry points and offers broader access to students with a wider range of prior content knowledge (Figure 5.1). Also, in this open-ended task, students are deepening their conceptual knowledge of other math concepts beyond area, including factors, multiples, fractions, and decimals. Notice that in the first version of the task, students simply are recalling the formula for the area of a rectangle and applying it. They are not deepening conceptual knowledge of any math concepts. As discussed in Chapter 4, the "recalling" and "applying" of the first task are low on Bloom's taxonomy. On the other hand, when students engage in the process of "creating" rectangles, "negotiating" assumptions, and "comparing" approaches in the second version, they are "evaluating" and "creating," which are on the top of the scale for strategies that promote higher-order thinking. In addition, a variety of reach zones (ZPDs) are accommodated with the second version.

While students are discussing, drawing, and creating rectangles in Boaler's mathematical mindset approach, instructors facilitate learning to deepen conceptual knowledge. Expert facilitation provides structure that minimizes extraneous load. Instructors do not confirm the correctness of students' answers. Instead, they ask questions like, "Why do you think that approach is a good idea?" "Could you tell me more about what you are thinking there?" "Why do you think that your group's answer is different than the other groups' answers?" "Could you tell us more about why you drew the problem out like that?" "How are your group's assumptions different than the other groups' assumptions?" If you are interested in a poster that demonstrates questions that instructors can ask to facilitate constructive conversations in math, please refer to Jeff Zwiers's Constructive Conversations Skills Poster at Understanding Language/Stanford Center for Assessment, Learning, and Equity (see jeffzwiers.org/tools).

THE NEUROSCIENCE BEHIND INTERACTIVE INQUIRY-BASED LEARNING

From a neuroscientist's perspective, learning occurs when neurons fire and new neural networks are formed. Accomplishing tasks that are progressively more complex creates stronger neural connections by capitalizing on neuroplasticity, the capacity of the brain to adapt and rewire itself. This suggests that the complex nature of interactive, inquiry-based learning generates strong neural networks, and thus optimizes learning potential.

Research indicates that: (1) complex approaches to learning foster the development of neural networks that promote long-term memory retrieval and (2) greater brain activity occurs as the complexity of problems increases. For example, elementary students engage in processes that are simultaneously neural and cognitive when learning arithmetic. Multiple regions of the brain are activated when they learn to add 3 + 7 (Menon, 2014). These neurocognitive processes facilitate (1) the learning of both new and increasingly more complicated problems, and (2) the storing of information in long-term memory (Menon, 2014). Long-term memories are stored in the brain in well-established networks of neurons that repeatedly fire together and therefore wire together. For example, 2nd graders who rely on multiple strategies to learn subtraction, rather than only memorization, perform better on math PSATs an entire decade later. When these high-PSAT performers complete arithmetic tasks, fMRI scans indicate that brain regions associated with memory retrieval are activated, signifying that they successfully transitioned from initial strategies to build well-established neural networks (Price, Mazzocco, & Ansari, 2013). Furthermore, Berteletti and Booth (2015) found that when young adults perform single-digit subtraction, the area of the brain associated with finger-counting is activated, suggesting that finger perception relates to math competency in adults. To assess finger perception, put your hand underneath the table and have someone touch a random finger. Can you easily identify which finger is touched? That is finger perception. One final fMRI study on reading indicates that when students use more complex phonetic approaches to learn reading rather than just memorizing sight words like *cat* or *dog,* they perform better in the subsequent grade (McCandliss, Beck, Sandak, & Perfetti, 2003). Similar results were found for adult beginning readers (Marian et al., 2007; Yoncheva, Wise, & Mc-Candliss, 2015). These studies support the idea that complex approaches to learning, like inquiry-based, group learning, create strong neural networks that optimize learning potential—even decades later.

Neuroscience studies about bilingualism also support the idea that working in groups and engaging in complex tasks contribute to greater neural activity and subsequent increases in neural networks, and thus learning. For example, a non-native English speaker in a math, physics, writing, English, or biology class will have to do a lot more cognitive processing to master the content. That student will be learning the content, while simultaneously learning vocabulary and concepts in a second language. Monolingual students have to master only the content knowledge. Therefore, bilingual students are building more neural connections than monolingual students as a result of engaging in more cognitively demanding tasks, and it is no surprise that bilingual students have greater executive functioning in some areas of the brain. For example, bilingual infants have greater abilities to infer (Addyman & Mareschal, 2013). Bilingual adults stave off the symptoms of Alzheimer's for an extra 5 years

Grouping Strategies and Group-Worthy Tasks

Usually, I group in pairs or groups of four. I have larger groups if I am doing a game show or debate, where one half of the class is interacting with the other half of the class. I let students know ahead of time that I randomly assign groups every week using an online random team generator. This way students get to know all of the other people in the class and get good at working with all kinds of people on a team, which is a 21st-century skill. Jerry Miller, senior dean of Career and Technical Education, says, "Nowadays employers have employees work in teams. Employers tell me, 'Send me the C student who can work with others in a group as opposed to the A student who can only work in a silo.'"

Rather than randomizing, one instructor, Carlos Valencia, allows groups to organize more organically. When he sees that certain groups are coalescing and exemplifying good group behaviors, he capitalizes upon it as a model for the rest of the class. Toward the end of the semester, I do a hybrid model of grouping where some days I let students choose their grouping and other times I assign groups. To hold students accountable for working in groups, I assign each group a number—and place the number on each group's desks. Therefore, I can say, "Group 1 will be presenting on the solution to the first word problem, Group 2 the second, etc." If I just ask, "Could someone in class tell me their approach?" sometimes I hear crickets—or worse, I hear from the same two students. If I tell a group that it will be presenting on something in a few minutes, the entire group will collaborate.

The key to doing amazing inquiry-based, interactive group-work is having high-leverage tasks, what *complex instruction* enthusiasts call group-worthy tasks (Cohen, Lotan, Scarloss, & Arellano, 1999). A carefully selected task will maximize the number of students learning in their reach zones (ZPDs), because it differentiates learning. Even if an instructor does not have much experience facilitating group discussions and inquiry-based learning, a group-worthy task will teach the instructor how to facilitate. However, it is not necessary to have a group-worthy task every single day.

Using some of the ideas in this book, maybe you can make an existing task even more impactful for students. Specific criteria exist for designing or selecting group-worthy tasks and activities. Two qualities that make tasks group-worthy are that they are open-ended, meaning there is not one correct solution, but multiple solutions; and that there is not one correct approach, but multiple correct approaches depending on assumptions a student makes. Even if a task or activity has one correct solution, a good task or activity allows for multiple approaches to complete it, so students can draw from their prior knowledge. In Ann's English activity, students have different clustering interpretations and descriptive outlines, and they are asked to articulate their assumptions and justifications for their choices. It is important for students to have opportunities to negotiate and justify their reasoning, approach, perspectives, and solutions. Another quality of a good task is that it has multiple entry points. For example, in the case of the rectangle task, students could start with any rectangle. In the case of the "What Is Art?" activity in Dan Munton's class, students could offer any thought that they came up with. One can see how a low-floor/high-ceiling task can accommodate a range of reach zones (ZPDs) of students.

In sum, group-worthy, high-leverage tasks have these qualities in common. They:

- invite students to communicate their unique approaches, perspectives, and reasoning
- are open-ended
- have low floors and high ceilings
- have multiple entry points and solutions
- have multiple ways to assess success
- involve conversations where students build on one another's knowledge
- require students to justify their reasoning, approaches, and assumptions
- activate students' prior knowledge
- have real-life applications

Here are some examples of group-worthy activities that I have used in the past: **conversation carousel,** peer feedback activities, **gallery walk, jigsaw reading and presenting, creating concept maps in groups, number talks,** debates, **Frayer model, merry-go-round,** and **gap cards.**

Open-Ended and Probing Questions

Open-ended and probing questions support inquiry-based learning. One of the advantages of the social constructivist approach to teaching is that the discussions make student learning more explicit. This, in turn, makes it easier to check for student understanding and to gather data to refine our instruction. To elicit expanded evidence of student learning, instructors ask probing and open-ended questions that push students to elaborate on their reasoning and justifications. The instructor can ask probing and open-ended questions to push students to investigate their reasoning more fully; to make learning more explicit; and to ultimately deepen conceptual understanding. "Why do you think that you got a different answer than the other group?" "What assumptions did your group make?" "Can you tell me more about what you were thinking here?" Probing and open-ended questions will prompt students to clarify, elaborate, and justify. They promote high-order thinking and are related to Bloom's "creating" category where instructors are prompting students to propose, negotiate, justify, report, or revise. Instructors focus not on correctness of answers, but instead on getting students to elaborate on their reasoning or perspectives.

Some open-ended, **probing questions** instructors use are:

- Why do you think this is the case?
- Why did you approach the solution that way?
- Why do you agree or disagree with that approach or way of thinking?
- Could you tell me a little bit more about what you were thinking here?
- Could you propose an alternative meaning, approach, solution?
- Could you tell me why this approach would or would not work?
- Can you show me how you arrived at your present conclusion?
- What would you have to change in order for . . . ?
- Where do you think you might be struggling the most?
- How might your assumptions influence your approach?
- How can you justify your reasoning?
- Can you generalize a pattern?
- Can you compare those two points of view?
- What is the muddiest point or the clearest point so far?

Scaffolding and Facilitating

Facilitating inquiry-based, interactive learning requires scaffolding learning for students. A good example of scaffolding is when Ann Foster does a think-aloud to model what students should be doing when analyzing the architecture of an essay. Ann scaffolds learning again when she starts students with an eight-paragraph essay and then gradually moves them toward analyzing longer and more complex essays. She carefully facilitates learning in groups as she moves them toward analyzing very complex essays independently. Ultimately, her careful scaffolding of a series of activities teaches students to write essays.

Lauralyn Larsen, an instructor in the Work Experience Department, uses scaffolded learning in her Career Development course. On the first day she posts a relevant quote or a video with a quote on a PowerPoint slide. She scaffolds the oral sharing of students' ideas in groups by having students do a 5-minute free-write before they talk about their ideas in small groups. This is a variation of the **think-pair-share** (TPS). Instead, it is a **think-write-pair-share.** After students have had time to organize their thoughts on paper, she has students present about their thoughts on the quote in pairs. After students have shared in pairs, she does **snowballing.** This is where students share out in a pair, then two pairs share out in a group of four. Then they may form a group of eight to share out with the whole class. Ultimately, she will build on these activities to scaffold the learning of the skills involved in job interviewing. She uses this series of activities to scaffold the teaching of interviewing skills for students by having them first develop their skills at writing, then share what they wrote in pairs, then share what they discussed in larger and larger groups. Since this is a course that teaches career skills, Lauralyn engages in this gradual-release model to get students talking comfortably about themselves, so eventually they will have the requisite skills to ace a job interview.

Dr. Michael Washington, author of Chapter 6 in this book, offers another example of scaffolding done in his U.S. history class. Michael writes "Freedom" on the board and asks students to think about what freedom means to them. Then students discuss their thoughts in pairs. Afterward, he facilitates a whole-class discussion based on the small-group conversations. This is basically a TPS activity—which is a scaffolding activity in and of itself. Still, Michael uses this tapping-into-prior-knowledge TPS activity as a springboard to discuss course content later. For example, when he covers the Civil War, he draws from these prior student conversations about freedom to talk about the more objective aspects of the Civil War and slavery.

Another example of scaffolding is a **conversation carousel.** I used this in a financial math class to launch discussions about credit. Also, I used it in a class for preservice teachers seeking to support English learners (ELs) as a culminating activity to synthesize and summarize learning. Whether as a launch or culminating activity, here is how it is done. You put up five statements on five posters around the room. It is better to use statements that are either controversial or common myths, in order to create more cognitive disequilibrium. For example, in the financial math class, I post, "The best way to pay off credit card debt is *always* to pay off the credit card with the highest interest first." In reality, the "best" way to pay off one's credit card debt depends on the individual situation; therefore, this statement sparks a lot of discussion about students' individual circumstances. In the education class, I post common myths about teaching EL education, like, "Exposing children to both English and their native language at home leads to delays in language acquisition in English," and "If students can converse with their peers in English, they can easily succeed academically." It is a pernicious misconception among educators that when they observe a bilingual student speaking fluent English in a conversation with peers, the student also can speak fluent academic English in a math or science class. It is difficult to get students to adapt their existing schemas to accommodate this idea. Therefore, it is a great statement to include in a conversation carousel.

In a conversation carousel, students work in groups of two, three, or four. Each group gets a number, 1–5. Each group places a Post-it on each poster about why students agree or disagree with the statement. Each group summarizes and presents on the poster's Post-it that corresponds to their group's number. Finally, I facilitate a whole-class discussion. In the financial math class, because I use it as a launch activity, the post-carousel activity is to read a report from FICO stating some facts about credit. Then we share out again as a class about what was surprising. In the education class, because I use the conversation carousel as a culminating activity, we use the post-carousel share-out to deepen conceptual knowledge with special focus on topics that students have yet to fully grasp in depth. Also, in the education class, students are encouraged to draw from the class readings to defend their positions on the posters. In both cases, the conversation carousel is used as a means to scaffold learning.

Some other scaffolding and facilitating activities and strategies are:

- using visual representations to illustrate student reasoning
- using Zwiers conversation posters to model constructive **conversations for students**
- using graphic organizers
- avoiding announcing your own point of view or confirming whether their approach or solution is correct
- **modeling using the fishbowl activity**

- modeling using role-play
- providing sentence frames for conversations
- providing index cards with starter and response questions for paired discussions
- **assigning group roles:** recorder, investigative reporter, timekeeper, facilitator, spy
- **philosophical chairs**
- **four corners**
- **facilitated brainstorming**
- explicitly teaching group-work skills (e.g., turn-taking, disagreeing, etc.)

Real-Life Connections

The last area to attend to when doing inquiry-based learning relates to making real-life connections. This section begins with a story from Jerry Miller, a first-generation college student and Senior Dean of Career and Technical Education. The following scenario underscores the importance of making real-life connections for students.

> When I was in my early 20s, I put myself through college. I was working for an engineer as a draftsperson, and I thought I really wanted to do that for a living. It was the 70s. I was working full-time and enrolled at SRJC in trig during the summer. I had never had trig in high school. I was struggling. . . . I was still struggling with math. I had gotten a D in geometry in high school . . . and I became a land surveyor. Now, what does a land surveyor do?! Well, they turn the entire world into a triangle!
>
> In 15 minutes, I learned trig. Why?. . . because the instructor pulled out a triangle and said, "You are looking at a plot of land. That's the elevation (Jerry motions as if he is talking about a hilltop in the distance) and that's the slope (Jerry gestures to me that he is walking up a hill)." That is not a hypotenuse! This instructor explained [trig] in terms that I understood. I said, Why didn't an instructor say that before?! The same thing is true in calculus. . . . The up and the down of a roadway is the tangent or a slope line and then it goes into a parabola. The minimum and the maximum are the second derivatives. Why didn't someone just say that the low points are where the water goes and erodes and the high point is where you have to see over on the top?! It was a real-life application. I was then able to understand the mathematical concepts. Why is it important to know statistics or error analyses? To make sure the construction is solid. We do not want things to break down and be unsafe.

Jerry's story is an example of how when instructors make explicit connections between the content and students' lived experiences, students learn better. In Jerry's example, an instructor drew from real-life applications to explain trigonometry concepts. This is similar to the example in Chapter 4, where a chemistry instructor taps into students' experiences in real life. She notices that her students persistently do not adapt their existing schema to fully accommodate the concept of whether substances do or do not require energy to change to a solid, liquid, or gas state. Therefore, she taps into their real-life experiences with water to ensure that they "get it."

Another way to connect the content to students' lives is to create or find real-life tasks, assignments, and activities that are relevant to their lived experiences, identities, and cultural backgrounds. In my study in the Yucatán, I created two real-life, open-ended, high-floor/low-ceiling math problems that students solved in groups. These problems were connected to real-life problems. They were radically different than the single-solution, single-method math problems students usually solved on worksheets in class. As described earlier, in this Yucatec Maya village motorcycle taxi drivers have no gas gauges or speedometers, yet they take innovative approaches to calculating mileage (Darling, 2017, 2019). Therefore, I created a math task, which asked students to "develop a plan to ensure a motorcycle taxi driver does not run out of gas." A second math task asked students to identify three social problems in the village and then design a community center to address these issues. Their design had specific constraints; it had to include a triangular shaped ecological area surrounded by rectangles. The goal was to get them to "discover" the Pythagorean formula—a topic that their instructor identified as challenging. Students really enjoyed working in groups to solve problems related to their real lives. Also, they persisted in solving the problems using innovative approaches. Dan Munton's "What Is Art?" activity also is based on students' real lives, because students draw from their own lived experiences about art to discuss the prompt.

In an example from an anthropology class, an instructor has students act as real anthropologists and interview people from their own social circles. In a psychology class, an instructor has students observe greetings and goodbyes in real life and take fieldnotes to investigate social mores. Students can do debates in a language class on topics germane to their own lives. Drawing from students' background experiences may be particularly relevant when the topic is a pernicious challenge for students to learn, for example, the Pythagorean formula in the Yucatec Maya math class.

In this section, we are talking about not just tapping into prior content knowledge, but also tapping into students' lived experiences: the sum of their identities, beliefs, and core values born out of their unique life circumstances. Of course, this requires that instructors lean in and peer into the lives of their students. In my study, I did a 6-month ethnography, so I knew a lot about the specific mathematical expertise in the community. In our classes, we may have to explicitly ask students who they are and what they are into, in order to become informed about their lived experiences. Also, we can read about different cultural groups, attend cultural events, and attend workshops. Because instructors are researchers and scientists, we engage in the cycle of instruction improvement. We continually experiment with how to best connect with students in meaningful ways and how to weave students' cultural assets and perspectives into instruction to improve learning opportunities for students. Interactive, inquiry-based instruction, in general, provides more opportunities for students to draw from their prior knowledge and lived experiences to construct new knowledge.

BUILDING A COMMUNITY OF LEARNERS

Another area to attend to when teaching inquiry-based, interactive learning relates to building a community of learners. Whether you deliberately create a community of learners or not, one is constructed by default in every classroom. However, it may not be a community of learners that supports the social constructivist approach to instruction. Maybe it is one where some students' voices are heard and others are not. Maybe it is one in which students do not co-construct knowledge, but rather are regarded as empty vessels into which the instructor pours objective knowledge. Maybe it is a community of learners where the instructor and textbook are the authorities in the room, and students' expertise is not valued and their prior knowledge is left untapped. Whether you do it with deliberation or not, some sort of classroom culture emerges in every class. Therefore, instructors may as well build one that serves all students in the most inclusive and equitable way. In this section I discuss: (1) what a community of learners is; (2) real instructors' strategies for the first day and first few weeks of class to build the community of learners; and (3) how to sustain an evolving community of learners.

The concept of *community of practice* originated with Lave and Wenger (1991). A community of practice describes a group of people "who share a concern, a set of problems, or a passion about a topic, and who deepen their knowledge and expertise in this area by interacting on an ongoing basis" (Wenger, McDermott, & Snyder, 2002, p. 4). The authors argue that those in the communities of practice determine the manner in which learning is constructed. McDermott (1993) echoes this idea: "Learning does not belong to individual persons, but to the various conversations of which they are a part" (p. 292). Instructors can form communities of practice to refine their craft, as well. Also, classrooms can serve as communities of practice for students as they develop mastery in a specific subject area. For example, students in a physics, math, or writing class form a community of practice to learn about physics, math, or writing. I prefer to use the phrase *community of learners* as it places people, rather than the practice, at the center.

Building a Community of Learners, the First Day

If you have been teaching for a while, then you probably have your favorite getting-to-know-each-other activity for the first day. Therefore, this section does not provide an exhaustive menu of those. Instead, it describes a few high-leverage/low-investment strategies that produce high yields in terms of building student connections and ultimately student outcomes.

Safety is an important facet of building a community of learners. All students should feel safe sharing their unique perspectives in the class. Lauralyn Larsen, Work Experience instructor, shares some first-day activities in her Career Development class to build a community of learners that values introverts. She may have a quiet class, where conversations and group activities can be difficult to start. On the first day, she immediately does a writing assignment so "students feel a sense of safety in sharing personal information," and she always gives students permission to pass when sharing in groups. This gives them time to think about what it is that they want to say before they have to share out verbally. Eventually she talks about the personality strengths of introversion. On the first day she says, "Some of you might like to think about it first before you talk about it," to give permission to those whose cognitive processing works best by thinking first, then speaking. She talks more about the differing communication styles of introverts and extroverts later in the course when she interprets the Myers-Briggs personality inventory. Helping students understand their differing and unique strengths in speaking in the classroom gives them more confidence and agency, and thus helps them to feel more welcome when they otherwise might be reluctant in a new community of learners.

Another strategy that Lauralyn employs on the first day is gathering background information on her students by asking them to write responses to prompts, including: "We all come from different backgrounds, is there anything special you want me to know about you . . . that you think I should know that could aid me in helping you?" She is surprised by what they share with her. They may share their disability. They may share trauma. One student shares, "I am homeless right now." Another shares, "I work 50 hours a week and I am afraid that I will fail." One student writes, "I am a Latina and my family does not support me going to college. My dad wants me to go to work." Then Lauralyn gives them permission to "share a safe thing" when they share out in groups or pairs. They hand these background information papers in to her, so she can get to know each student early in the semester. Again, we hear the focus on safety for all students in Lauralyn's classes as she builds a community of learners.

I develop norms together with students on the first day. I do the "What do you like/not like while working in groups?" norm-building activity. I co-develop class norms with students along four domains: (1) technology use in class; (2) group-work; (3) lateness/tardiness; and (4) academic mindsets. Students work in groups of four to discuss norms around the first three areas. Then I scribe their ideas on the board. I frame the discussion around norm building in terms of *professional academic behavior*. I explain, "In regular life, I drop the F-bomb a lot. However, that kind of language is not appropriate for a professional academic environment, so I code-shift and do not use that language here in the classroom." Some giggle a bit at that. I frame the discussion of norms like this to emphasize the fact that there is nothing wrong with their own home or cultural vernacular. It is just that this professional academic environment requires some code-switching—even for me. When we talk about technology, I discuss how they are the technology generation and have a lot of experience with using technology in many settings. I tell them that it is their job is to educate me about what technology use looks like in a professional academic environment. When we build norms, usually the class echoes what I think about the use of cell phones and being late and absent. However, it is more powerful for them to hear their own voices in the development of norms.

Building a Community of Learners, the First Two Weeks

Rafael Vasquez, instructor and coordinator of an Extended Opportunity Program and Services (EOPS), shares what he does in his classes to develop a community of learners. EOPS connects students who may be ex-incarcerated, recently migrated, or living in poverty to resources. Rafael was a low-income, first-generation college student himself, so he easily connects with students. In addition, he provides enlightened leadership to the Latinx community both on campus and in the greater Santa Rosa, CA, area. He has a radio show, Lideres del Futuro (Leaders of the Future) on the bilingual station KBBF FM, 89.1. After interviewing him, I kind of felt like he was a real superhero, but instead of wearing a big red cape, he dons a long ponytail. The following paragraph describes what he does on the first day of a Latin American Studies course to build a community of learners.

> My goal in the classroom is always to empower all students to be able to feel that they have the same opportunity to participate, to share their information . . . even if I disagree with it. . . . That's the other thing. The first day of class, I always tell students I am not the teacher and you are not the students. We need to shift that mentality. You are my colleague and I am your colleague. And you have as much to teach me as I hopefully have to teach you in this class. I welcome any feedback and if you would like to challenge my knowledge on the subject, you are welcome to do so. I will go and re-read and we can dialogue about it.

He says that he is about empowering the students to think that they have something to say. There is evidence that his approach is working. Throughout the semester, he responds to student input with, "Let's listen to what our colleague has to say here." By the 9th week of the semester, the students are referring to each other as "colleague": "Well, my colleague over here is saying this and my colleague over there is saying that." He talks about a student who raised his hand last semester and said, "I am sorry. I disagree with you (Rafael) about this point"—and the student presented his point about the Mashika people and Montezuma. Rafael queried the class, "How many people agree or disagree with our colleague?" Most of the students did not know whether to agree or disagree with him; they did not have enough information on the topic. Rafael said, "I agree with your point of view, but I did not present enough on it. I will have us all read another article on the topic." This is an example of a student feeling empowered enough to challenge the instructor's perspective, respectfully. Rafael tries to create a "healthy space for students to voice their opinions without fear of grade reprisals because they disagree with you." Rafael assigned Chapter 2 of Paulo Freire's book, *The Pedagogy of the Oppressed* (2000). He continues:

> The book discusses the idea that students are like waste baskets. You throw the knowledge in and when you give them a test, you extract it out. That is not learning. It is called the banking concept of education. We talk about this in class and this gives more power to the idea of us being colleagues. I tell them, "I have been given the privilege to assign a grade, but the goal is for you to walk out of here with more knowledge than you came in with."

Another strategy that Rafael employs that contributes to building a community of learners is to play music for 5 minutes before every class begins. The music serves three functions. First, "students can transition in a healthy way to the material that we are going to present." Second, the music scaffolds the content in his lessons. Rafael gains 5 instructional minutes by playing music *before* class officially starts. He plays music that is related to the course content and then he alludes to the music to make explicit connections to the course content for that day. For example, when they talked about Argentina in his Culture and Values in Latin America and the Caribbean class, he played the music of Mercedes Sosa, a Grammy Award–winning Argentine singer. He used that music as a springboard to spark the conversation about what is happening in Argentina. He asked, "Remember what she said in the song?" In the Humanities in the U.S. course, he plays Tupac Shakur's song "Dear Mama" about his complex relationship with his mother, drugs, and poverty. This serves as the foundation to talk about one of the course topics, "the causation between poverty and criminality as a way of survival." The third purpose of the music is to connect to students' prior knowledge and cultural identities. Frequently, students can relate to the music played, as many of his students are aged 18 to 25 and are students of color or Latinx students. The music is working. In the feedback section of his course, in response to, "How can I improve my teaching skills?" students frequently say, "I love the music. It helps me transition to the course from my work or wherever I was coming from."

Another instructional approach Rafael recommends is to lean in and listen to where students are coming from, and connect their backgrounds to the content. Let them have the opportunity to share their stories. He says:

Dan Munton [math instructor] is the perfect example. What did Dan do? He went on a sabbatical to Guatemala and learned about the Maya and Spanish. Just because you teach math does not mean you cannot connect it to different people's cultures. Dan presented on it for Latinx students and he integrates it into his math courses. He taught Latinx students to be proud of their ethnic backgrounds in connection to math. Regardless of the course material, you can connect it to students' cultures. You can draw from students' expertise. Connect experiences to their lived experiences *and* to their historical identities. Dan taught Latinx students to be proud of their culture.

Claude Goldenberg, Stanford professor emeritus of education, brings leaning in and listening to students to the level of an art. In class, he would accurately paraphrase complex and idiosyncratic ideas that students expressed, and translate them for the entire class. He explains *back channeling*, the verbal and nonverbal cues that we communicate to a speaker that indicate we are listening intently. Claude says, "What you're communicating by back channeling . . . when you say nothing and instead listen intently . . . there's the relatively obvious advantage that you might learn something you didn't know; but then, perhaps, the not so obvious advantage is that you are communicating something important." Sometimes, I listen very hard, but still do not fully grasp a student's contribution. I tell the student, "I cannot quite understand your reasoning right now, but bring it back into the discussion later, because I sense there are some important points there that I do not quite comprehend yet."

Memorizing Names

Another high-leverage strategy for building a community of learners is memorizing students' names. Memorizing names is not just about memorizing names; it is about connecting to build a community of learners. I had a fixed mindset about my ability to memorize students' names and became resigned to the idea that I just could not do it. However, I used ideas from math instructors Carlos Valencia and Dan Munton and was successful.

Carlos invites students to sit wherever they want on the first day of class. Then he passes around a blank seating chart, and students write in their names. He asks students to sit in those seats for a couple of weeks. He tells students, "Hey, I'm doing this because it's really important for me to know you. Maybe during class, I might stare at you a really long time. That's only because I'm trying to remember your name." He brings the seating chart home to visualize students' faces.

Carlos noticed a major improvement in the tone of his class, attendance, and lateness, partly because when students return to class after being absent, he says, "Hi, Martin, I am so glad you are back. We missed you." Also, he noticed an increase in the number of students who were on time and in the number of students who came to his office and who asked for advice at the end of the semester about future enrollment in courses.

The tone in Dan Munton's class improved, as well. To memorize students' names by the end of his second week, Dan arrives to the first class 30 minutes early and asks students, "What is your name? Have you read a good book? Have you seen a movie lately?" He continues on the break and after class. For the first 2 weeks, he says each student's name every single day. He knows three-quarters of the names by the end of the first week and then he backslides a bit on the Monday of the second week. By the end of the second week, he knows all students' names. Dan is a self-admitted "geographical learner." He memorizes students' names by remembering where they sit. He says, "It is great when they sit in the same seat, but it is harder to memorize the names of students who move around." He goes on, "If students know that I know their name, then they are accountable and they know they are a person to me. They know that I took the time to know who they are." Another strategy is an optional extra credit assignment. Students can visit him in his office for 5 minutes during the first 2 weeks and tell him "something about yourself that is non-subject-related." Two other strategies are to offer extra credit if students upload their photos onto the course website and to have students make index cards on which they write their names.

Memorizing names is investing in relationships with students. Last semester I memorized my students' names by Week 2, and there was a radical shift in tone throughout the semester. By the end of the first class, students knew other students' names; helped each other with problems in the lab, and called me "Felicia." On the last day of the semester when I was doing the congratulatory handshakes, dozens of students surprised me by making very touching comments and giving me hugs.

Community Is Messy

Instructor Audrey Schell once said, "Building a community of learners can be messy." Instructors and students co-construct learning communities together. While there are key instructor moves to do on the first day and during the first week, it requires ongoing dialogue and compassion when mistakes are made. If you set the stage for this, your classroom culture will continue to blossom.

This section discusses challenges I experienced when building a community of learners. In the first example, I was teaching a pre-algebra course that was about 85% Latinx students. Karen and Maddie were 18 years old and White, and they frequently came to class late. On this day, they were particularly late, and they were working with the only Black student, Tamara, in a group of three. They kept leaning in and whispering and giggling, and Tamara looked alienated. We were doing the **merry-go-round activity,** where each group creates four short math problems that the next group in the merry-go-round has to solve. When I went over to their group, Karen and Maddie were off-task, not following directions, and continuing to laugh and exclude the third person in the group. Finally, I said, "I want you two to leave." They left. I followed up with an email about exhibiting professional academic behavior in future classes. When they came back to the next class, I felt like they were at risk of being ostracized by other class members. I made a point to illuminate their assets better during class. I felt like I had failed them by being so short with them in class and not pulling them in earlier. For the rest of the semester, when I noticed strong professional academic behaviors, I would comment, "Karen, your attendance has been great." "Maddie, can you explain that to the class? That is a really innovative approach." "Thanks for helping Juan with that problem." "Karen, you really leaned in today in your group-work." They became great assets to the classroom culture. They came on time, contributed a lot in small-group discussions, and performed very well on assessments. This is an example where I was able to bring students back into the fold of the community by illuminating their assets. Communities are forgiving, if the instructor models forgiveness.

In the second example, a non-Latinx student, Magrit, came to class on the second day of my bilingual (Spanish/English) financial math class. Most students had jobs, were Latinx, and were between the ages of 35 and 50. During the first class, I established the norm that students could speak either language and I would scaffold language to make it work for everyone. Some students wanted to improve their Spanish, others their English. When Magrit came on the second day, I spoke Spanish and English as I had done on the first day. About 10 minutes into the second class, Magrit blurted out, "This class is confusing, because of all that Spanish." I responded, "The PowerPoints and handouts are translated into both languages." When I passed out papers, I asked students whether they wanted the English or Spanish version, or both. When I asked Magrit, she shouted, "English of course. I only speak English." She said it in a way that implied, "D'uh!" Up to this point in the class, at any random moment, about 90% of the students were speaking Spanish or Spanish/English.

Suddenly, Magrit announced to the whole class, "Everybody here should be speaking English! Everybody here has a job! They should be speaking English at that job! Plus (looking at me) your Spanish is not even that good." No one gave any indication that they even noticed what she said, but a remarkable thing happened—the class was no longer bilingual. The entire class began speaking English instead of Spanish. The one monolingual Spanish speaker had stopped talking altogether. It was like a dagger had been plunged into the heart of this community of learners.

No instructor is ever totally prepared for this kind of threat to the classroom culture. As the authority in the classroom, I spoke immediately to preserve that feeling of safety in the room for everyone. I said, without equivocation, "We live in a bilingual society. This class is bilingual. I was hired to teach a bilingual class. I am going to ask students what works best for them in terms of language. I want your opinion, Magrit, and everyone else's, too. I want to make instruction work for the whole classroom community, every single person in this room." Like a wave, Spanish language filled the airways again. At the end of class I spoke to Magrit privately. I did not directly address the comments that she made in class. Instead I said, "I am so happy that you are in this class. Thank you for asking really good questions that maybe others feel uncomfortable asking. Also, I love what you had to offer about budgeting food in the **gallery walk** activity."

On the third day of class, Magrit came early and I continued to communicate that I valued her input. "Remember those grocery-buying tips you mentioned last week. I was able to cut $300 off my grocery budget. Thanks! We are lucky to have you in class. I hope you get to share more of your ideas with the entire class. I think you have a lot more to share than you realize." During class I praised Magrit publicly and asked her to share her unique budgeting ideas with the class. By the fifth week, she had made long-term friendship bonds with some of the bilingual students in class. Sometimes people lash out in class because they are scared or feel like they don't belong. It is important to act swiftly to reassure the whole class that the classroom is a safe environment, and then follow up with vocal students to reassure them that they are also valued members of the class. Sometimes students who act like bullies are just scared of being excluded themselves.

A third example involves a very different kind of challenge. Sometimes it takes a lot of work to generate the glue to keep a community of learners together. In this example, I talk about options for sustaining a community when the glue becomes too strong. In Fall 2017, students in my class really gelled. They loved working in groups during class. I felt very respected by them and connected to them. From their newly minted in-class liaisons emerged outside-of-class friendships. Many students formed study groups and worked together on homework in the math lab outside of class. Some came to class with stories about how their new friendships were blossoming at parties and other outings. This class came to be a tightly knit community of learners. However, disaster struck when the Santa Rosa area was hit by a series of tragic fires that destroyed 6,800 buildings. Many students and faculty lost their homes, were evacuated, or experienced other tragic losses. As a result, SRJC cancelled classes for 2 weeks. When we returned to class after the fires, I brought in pastries, facilitated a conversation about the tragedy, and continued to support students who lost homes. However, I noticed a drastic change. Students who previously were class leaders were derailing others to be off-task in class and disregarded my attempts to bring the class content and goals back into focus. Their behavior came off as very disrespectful. Apparently, students had spent the 2 weeks off developing tighter bonds with their newly found friends. I was telling Ellen Shick, English instructor, about this sudden shift in class behavior. She said that it sounds like "hyper-bonding." Thank goodness for collegial collaborations; she saved our class. Watts (2013) describes hyper-bonding as "a disruptive force in the learning community characterized by non-productive student behaviors, group absenteeism, disrespect shown toward the instructor, off-task conversations during lecture or lab time, inappropriate dominance over class discussions, and other unruly behaviors." It is particularly common when there are cohorts of students, because they forge out-of-class liaisons (Hubbell & Hubbell, 2010).

To address this issue, first I identified what was wrong. My class had hyper-bonded. Second, I spoke to the class directly about professional academic behavior. I pulled out the slide from an earlier session and went over what this means and reminded them about the implicit contract that we had around these norms. Third, I addressed the idea directly that this class did a great job of building relationships during the break to support one another. Still, it was important that they continued to support their peers' success in this class, by supporting others' educational and career goals. I think the students wanted a way out, too. They really needed guidance from an authority figure to get back to their previous roles of being participants in a constructive learning community. Within a day, their behavior changed back to the previous, productive group behavior. Another strategy to address hyper-bonding is to reinsert yourself into the relationships with students. Have them do a reflection that they share with only you. Also, you could facilitate a structured, graded group activity to reel them in from becoming so off-task in group conversations. If you feel that there are a couple of high-status students who dominate conversations that veer other students away from the course content, meet with the high-status students to tell them that they are leaders and that you would like them to use those leadership skills to help other students learn the content so they can all be successful.

A fourth example deals with the challenge of building a community with quieter students. Valuing the contributions of introverts is also a part of building a community of learners. Every class is different. I described a class that was so extroverted that it hyper-bonded. On the other end of the spectrum, I had a class that was so introverted that I had to adapt my instruction, the physical classroom environment, and my communication approach to create an interactive community of learners. Part of creating a strong community of learners is illuminating the assets of all students in the classroom. An instructor may say, "You contribute a lot in groups." "You ask good probing questions." However, how do we shine the light on the contributions of introverts in the classroom? This is part of building a community of learners. In this pre-algebra class of 22, only one or two students regularly would share their ideas in large-group discussions, ask questions, or present on the board. They all took good notes, though. The classroom was cramped, had those desks that are welded to the chairs, and the chairs were not on wheels. It was difficult to move around. In my other classes, if I provided prompts for discussion to launch a topic or gave a group-worthy problem to work on, groups would effortlessly engage in discussions. In this class, they would discuss only if I explicitly said, "Now compare your solution with the person to the right of you." "Now, discuss with that person why you think that your approach is conceptually sound."

Things were getting desperate in this quiet class. Also, students were not doing as well in this class as students in the other sections of the course were doing. I made a room change in the fourth week to a classroom that had: large oval tables that seated four; comfortable chairs on wheels; and a lot of room to move around. I recommend securing rooms that are more conducive to group-work, whenever possible. It was re-markable how changing rooms transformed the classroom dynamic. For the first time, this class scored higher than the other sections on a quiz. For the first time, Maria offered to come up to the document camera to share her answers even though some of them might be wrong. In a pre-vious class, I asked her to come to the board and she flatly said, "No." Suddenly students were sharing their approaches with the whole class.

Susan offered her work on the document camera even though it had errors, and she loved the idea that she got the extra attention of getting help from the class with her errors. A few weeks later she said, "I hat-ed working in groups, but being in this class made it not so bad." It is not uncommon to hear students who are more introverted say that they do not like working in groups. Susan's buy-in was an important get for the classroom culture. In fact, Susan was the first one to begin secretly communicating with me with her fingers under her desk to indicate her answers. This prompted me to emphasize more nonverbal checking-for-understanding strategies for this group. For example, I invited students to put up fingers to communicate how well they understood the material (one finger for not much and five for they totally got it) or to indicate which number was correct.

This class of more introverted students also made me realize that I need to explicitly recognize the work of introverts in the classroom and when they are working in groups. I am always thanking students for ask-ing questions that benefit everyone, and for taking risks by coming up to the board to justify their reasoning. However, I began saying, "Thank you if you are an introvert. Thanks to everyone who is watching really hard and listening deeply. These efforts really affect the success of group-work, because you are bringing this careful attention to detail to solving the problems that we do in groups." Many students lit up in this new classroom environment.

The fifth example is about lateness and other circumstances out-side of the classroom. Lateness is a pernicious problem plaguing com-munities of learning at community colleges. I offer three strategies in this section. First, I facilitate a discussion about lateness when we co-develop group norms the first day. Second, as we move along and are building a community of learners, I explain how everyone's behavior affects the group: "When you are late or unprepared, it affects everyone in your group and in the classroom." I don't humiliate students who are late. However, sometimes I will speak individually to a student who is habitually late. Each student I get to come to class on time helps to build this practice in others. Sometimes I will put up a slide in the fifth week to remind students about professional academic behavior and the participation points they earn or do not earn when they are on time or late. Third, I begin most classes saying, "Thanks for coming today and being on time."

In the middle of the semester, if there is a movement toward increasing latecomers, I do an intervention. In Fall 2017, I gave students who were there on time a super-secret hint about the next quiz, which the latecomers did not get. When the late students finally came in, I directly told the class that everyone should come on time and why I was irritated by this behavior. It is important not to direct this kind of scolding to the whole class unless you have communicated to those who are on time beforehand that you are not talking to them. Otherwise it can have a demotivating effect.

Sometimes extra tending to the community of learners is required because of looming outside forces. This scenario happened during the semester after the big Santa Rosa fires. Many of my students were beleaguered by the flu or were suffering from the aftermath of the fires. Also, I had undocumented students who were just plain fearful because of welling anti-immigrant sentiment in the United States. Students looked fatigued, haggard, demoralized, and crestfallen. At the beginning of this semester, two students had been hospitalized because of the flu and had to drop the course. I felt like my students were dreading coming to class, but I did not feel like it was about me or this pre-algebra class in particular.

Consequently, I asked each student as students trailed into class, "Do you think the fires, the flu, and the political tension on campus and the United States are affecting the overall campus culture?" Tia said, I definitely think there is a vibe shift on campus right now." Maya said, "I had to work 12 days in a row, because there are only a few employees left to work at my job since the fires." Yasmin said, "I am now seeing an immunologist." It is hard enough for students who already juggle work, family, and school. Also, many of my students are undocumented, and they were singed from the anti-immigrant sentiment that was heating up on the national level. I told students that I wanted to give them a break, so I brought a bag of candy to class and I let them work on a unit practice test in class instead of assigning it for homework. Also, I told them, "Today, find people who love you and care about you and spend some time with them. These are tough times." For the first time in weeks, Lisa and Paulo worked really hard in the lab.

I have learned to tote around a bag of candy for those challenging moments. Also, I keep available some academic concessions that I am willing to make in order for students to feel the boost of a generous moment. For example, sometimes I grant students an extension on a particular assignment that I know comes at a tough time in the semester. Or maybe I allow them to use class time on an assignment that normally would be homework, so they can get help from me. One time, I gave students in my 8 A.M. class three points on their unit test, because it was on the morning of daylight savings time and a student showed me research about how daylight savings time affects students' grades. Their tired little faces lit up when I told them that. The bottom line is that many students are overworked and tired, and a little generosity and compassion go a long way toward building a community of learners.

CHAPTER 6

Improving Retention and Engagement for First-Year Black Male Students in Higher Education

Michael L. Washington

By the time the student uttered the sentence "I love learning; I hate school," not only was I not shocked; I was expecting it.

—Susan Blum (2016)

I begin this chapter with these profound words of revelation as they also are befitting of a particular college demographic that often is underserved and misunderstood: the Black male college student.

Although it's true that African Americans have achieved academic gains in recent decades, it's also true that significant gaps persist when compared with their ethnic peers, especially regarding Black *males* (Shapiro et al., 2017; Washington, 2013). It's also important to point out that other ethnic and marginalized populations have faced similar challenges. From this perspective, all of these groups are considered to be marginalized; however, they all experience marginalization differently.

The problem is that in many educational institutions, Black males are treated as if they are *less* deserving, *less* welcome, and *less* capable of scholarship, or as if they are *invisible*, and therefore inconsequential. It is exactly these circumstances that contribute to Black males being viewed as an invading force on campus, or as a virtually "invisible" part of society, especially by other students and school personnel unfamiliar with, or uninterested in, their academic advancement (Lee & Ransom, 2011; Parker, Puig, Johnson, & Anthony, 2016). In this chapter, we examine some of these cultural and academic challenges as well as common behaviors demonstrated by Black male college students.

DISCUSSING MARGINALIZATION

When it comes to discussing why disproportionate percentages of Black male students are experiencing so many academic shortcomings, the search for causes often begins with the educational institutions themselves. Some examples of ongoing issues that exist within higher education are: increasing educational costs, concerns regarding standardized and culturally biased testing, ensuring appropriate academic rigor, the gradual shift toward hiring non-tenure adjunct faculty and instructors instead of tenure track faculty, the discontinuance of educational cohorts designed to accommodate working and marginalized students, and concerns regarding diversity initiatives and academic governance. These are all issues that affect all students, including Black males, and that faculty and administrators attempt to resolve regularly. However, for Black males, the challenges typically are influenced by socioeconomic and psychosocial phenomena that uniquely shape how Black males are perceived within our society as well as our educational institutions (Okamato, 2010; Werwath, 2016).

Despite these factors, Black males still must find a way to navigate through educational systems that tend not to favor either their race or their gender. Regarding race, the stereotype of Black males as dangerous "Black thugs," or egocentric "Black athletes," or the "dumb Black kids from the ghetto" often comes to mind. Black thugs, arrogant athletes, and poor Blacks from ghettos do exist, but often in the minority, not the majority. As a result of these misconceptions, an "uphill" battle begins from the first time Black children set foot in a preschool classroom and continues through college and grad school.

After the conclusion of the Civil War, African Americans never received their "40 acres and a mule." This begs the question: How can you pull yourself up by your bootstraps if you have no boots? In an attempt to meet Black male undergraduates "halfway," I encourage instructors to at least make an effort to learn and understand some of the history and culture of African Americans. You don't need to learn 400 years of Black history; just watch the news and pay attention to what's happening on campus and in your communities. Make an effort to have conversations with Black males in and out of your classrooms, not just about academics, but about them. You don't have to wait for Black male students to approach you. You can initiate the conversation and allow them to recognize your interest in them. This prevents Black males from becoming invisible and may encourage them to open up when they face challenges.

Acknowledging the existence of marginalization and racial privilege, as well as engaging in discourse, are key to improving education systems in a pluralistic society. This, in turn, will minimize or close achievement, graduation, and opportunity gaps for Black males in higher education.

INSTITUTIONAL CHALLENGES: RACIAL DEMOGRAPHICS

The statistical data regarding academic performance by African American students from K–16 to postsecondary education have been available for decades. The disparities are well documented in peer reviewed academic journals and government reports; however, gradual systemic changes are more evident in recent years. Though the percentage of Black students attending college in 2016 rose from 11.7% to 14.1% since 2000, achievement gaps and graduation gaps of Blacks compared to Whites, as well as Asians, remain virtually the same. Despite these statistical gaps, more Blacks are enrolled in college today than ever before, with an increase from 30.5% in 2000 to 34.9% in 2015 (Musu-Gillette et al., 2016).

In terms of graduation rates, according to a report by the National Center for Education Statistics (Musu-Gillette et al., 2016), in 2013, Blacks had the lowest overall graduation rate for first-time, full-time undergraduate students who started their postsecondary education at a 4-year school. Their graduation rate was 41%, compared with a national average of 59%, and 71% for Asian students (the highest score), based on a 6-year graduation rate at public 4-year institutions. For students attending community colleges, the percentages were even lower, with Black students achieving an 11% graduation rate for first-time, full-time students at a public 2-year institution in 2013, compared with the highest percentage by Asian students at 28%, over a 3-year time frame. This is unsettling considering that African Americans enroll at community colleges in higher percentages than White and Asian students, who have higher enrollment rates at 4-year institutions than African Americans. Blacks fare a little better when we look at 2-year degree rates overall among Americans aged 25 to 64. While only 22.6% of Latinx students possess a 2-year degree, 30% of Blacks and 47% of Whites possess a 2-year degree (NCES, 2018a).

STEM fields (science, technology, engineering, and math) have been promoted by both 2-year and 4-year colleges for quite some time as a means of developing employment skills and supporting advanced economies for the 21st century. Despite this demand, Blacks still do not partici-

Table 6.4. Six-Year Completion Rates for Undergraduate Students Who Started at 4-Year Public Institutions, by Race and Ethnicity (N = 1,236,815)

Race/Ethnicity	Completion Rate
Asian	71.7%
White	67.2%
Hispanic	54.9%
Black	45.9%

Table 6.5. Six-Year Dropout Rates for Undergraduate Students Who Started at 2-Year Public Institutions, by Race and Ethnicity (N = 1,089,776)

Race/Ethnicity	Dropout Rate
Asian	32.0%
White	41.5%
Hispanic	44.8%
Black	56.7%

Table 6.6. Six-Year Dropout Rates for Undergraduate Students Who Started at 4-Year Public Institutions, by Race and Ethnicity (N = 1,236,815)

Race/Ethnicity	Dropout Rate
Asian	14.2%
White	21.4%
Hispanic	27.1%
Black	35.3%

siliency. Duckworth's research is commendable, however, its applications may not necessarily be universal. Duckworth's foundational research was conducted primarily with privileged populations, such as Ivy League undergraduates, West Point cadets, and high-achieving contestants in the National Spelling Bee, not with truly marginalized populations. Shortly after grit theory was popularized, anti-grit narratives began to surface. Several concerns within this community are directly linked to Black males in postsecondary education (Goodman & Fine, 2018; Perry, 2016).

Institutional Accountability

Based on Duckworth's grit theory, instead of having educational institutions examine their own practices and policies, or hold themselves accountable for any inadequacies, students who face challenges would be expected to use grit as a means of overcoming the challenges on their own. This essentially lets educational institutions "off the hook" regarding flaws within the system and sets a precedent for other institutions to follow suit. In these circumstances, Black male undergraduates seeking support and understanding during their transition from secondary school to higher education might be denied much-needed assistance and could be expected to "pull themselves up by their bootstraps" when facing unequal or inequitable learning conditions compared with more privileged or socially and culturally advantaged students.

This perspective also promotes a mindset that *there are no excuses*, and that students essentially are the sole determinant of their own academic outcomes, regardless of cultural differences, social imbalances, and inequities. This feeds into racist stereotypes of Black males lacking the ability to compete academically with ethnic majorities.

Inherent Grit

Duckworth maintains that grit can be developed by students who lack it, as a means of overcoming adverse conditions within educational systems. However, there is a growing body of work that suggests that most marginalized students raised in at-risk environments may already possess grit. Based on current literature, this is especially true of Black male students. Disproportionate percentages of African American males live below the poverty line and often are considered to be the breadwinners in the family or the head of the household, even as teenagers. As a result of these trying conditions, they probably developed grit at an early age.

There are also a number of academic challenges that Black males encounter in grades K–16, such as a lack of access to advanced placement (AP) and gifted and talented education courses in K–12, and a lack of engagement and retention of Black males on college campuses (Harper, 2009). It is these lifelong experiences from birth to adulthood that many marginalized Black males encounter that are not the exception; they are often the norm. As a result, grit development is an inherent aspect of growing up for many Black males, who may have exercised some aspect of it just to gain entrance to college in the first place.

Based on this mindset, Black males in college don't need grit; they need understanding, support, and culturally critical engagement. They also need accountability from caring and culturally competent faculty and administrators, not "grittiness." Duckworth's grit theory can be quite useful for students who don't possess the tenacity and passion necessary for overcoming seemingly insurmountable odds. However, current anti-grit narratives suggest that middle- to upper-class majority ethnicities may not need grit because they usually have the necessary support systems and finances available to them, while marginalized populations may already possess the grit necessary to stay the course.

SOCIOLOGICAL CHALLENGES

College campuses often are viewed as inviting and comfortable social environments that promote intellectual and social interaction, as well as creativity and freedom of expression. For ethnic and cultural majorities, this has always been the case; however, for ethnic and cultural minorities, college campuses can be uninviting and, in some instances, even hostile. Despite the best of intentions, terms like *racism* and *White privilege* often alienate faculty and administrators, as well as students, and tend to influence defensive postures that are counterproductive in addressing the existence of issues that Black males do not have the luxury of ignoring.

Color-Blind Racism

One of the challenges Black male college students encounter is "color-blind racism" (Alexander, 2012; Mueller, 2017), a post–civil rights era form of racism that invalidates the racial identities of Blacks with the claim that those exercising it "don't see color." In the process, it allows those exercising it to deny people their racial identity, which inhibits racial progress in an effort to take "race" off the table.

Color-blind racism also creates a disconnect between cultures, which is detrimental to both Black and Whites, and can interfere in tracking racial disparities that exist within social systems and institutions. If race is not acknowledged as a factor in educational outcomes, then it becomes impossible to track or acknowledge racial inequities and disparities that exist within educational institutions themselves (Mueller, 2017). This racial ideology ultimately promotes selective ignorance and suggests that what makes African American culture unique from other cultures has become invisible or homogenized into some monolithic perspective of African American people.

Color-blindness is often disingenuous and may make it much easier for someone to turn a blind eye to racial injustices experienced by Blacks on and off campus. Color-blind racism isn't always verbalized. It can manifest itself as a form of nonverbal action or inaction. Silence also can be used as a means of becoming "color mute" in order to avoid being pulled into a discussion or circumstances that offer an opportunity to speak out on racial oppression. This is a major contributor to the continued existence of systemic racism.

Black Misandry

Another challenge Black males face in our society is "Black misandry" (Smith, Mustaffa, Jones, Curry, & Allen, 2016; Smith, Yosso, & Solórzano, 2007), a hatred or dislike specifically of Black boys and men. The catalyst for this hatred is usually fear, miseducation, or misinformation regarding Black males. American history is full of negative stereotypes regarding Black males, and most of those perspectives still exist today and are promoted via social media, television, radio, and other means of communication. The image of Black males as lazy, violent, stupid, devious, dirty, untrustworthy, evil, gang members, drug dealers and drug users, thieves, rapists, sub-humans or animals, and threats to society still shapes public opinion and reaction to the presence of Black males, largely to their detriment.

Black misandry is also a contributing factor in discriminatory hiring practices and housing policies, disproportionate K–12 school suspension rates, racial profiling, conscious and unconscious *racial priming* (early indoctrination of socialization promoting negative racialized messages), disproportionate incidents of excessive force by peace officers, the denigration of Black boys and men, as well as the practice of inequitable or discriminatory education policies.

Faculty or administrators who are guilty of exercising either color-blind racism or Black misandry could be placing the college at risk of violating several local, state, or federal laws and regulations. These incidents may seem harmless to some students or employees. Unfortunately, what begins as a slip of the tongue, or a snide remark, can quickly escalate into a campus-wide issue that could result in damaging the reputation of the institution, as well as suspending faculty and even the dismissal of employees.

more important, the students are engaged with the instructor and with one another.

Instructors act more as facilitators and allow the conversation to develop using a few basic guidelines. This form of engagement allows brainstorming and questions everything so as to eliminate contradictions and to develop theories for future examination (transitioning from theory to praxis). Desks or chairs can be arranged in groups or a circle or any fashion that de-emphasizes the educator as being the center of attention or being in a position of power. Socratic dialogue changes the focus from being teacher-centered to being student-centered and, if done properly, engages everyone in the room.

Practicing Mutual Accountability

Why don't instructors ask their students more often what the students expect of the instructor and hope for from the course? Some of their answers can surprise us. Asking what students expect holds us accountable to their needs. This doesn't mean that instructors are giving up power, but rather that they are establishing a sense of mutual accountability. The syllabus establishes what students are accountable for. Asking what students expect is a balance of accountability. It's in asking this question that the instructor's sense of accountability is established with students.

I also recommend a 3- to 5-minute feedback session once a week, at the end of class, to get basic feedback from students regarding what does or doesn't work in the classroom. This kind of immediate feedback allows the instructor to address issues in *real time* instead of waiting until the end of the semester to receive student feedback after the course has ended, when it's too late to apply their recommendations.

Being Genuine

My last recommendation is to be *genuine*. Earlier in this chapter we talked about double consciousness as it pertains to the duality of the lived experiences of Black male undergraduates. As faculty members or administrators, it's not unusual for us to wear many hats and to take on several responsibilities. Even if we're multitasking and addressing several issues in a class full of culturally diverse students who have different needs, it is critical that we find a way to be genuine—to be yourself, to not pretend, or act for the sake of others. The instructor needs to be honest first with herself, so that she can then be honest with students.

Some students are experienced "lie detectors" and can tell if an instructor is being sincere, and is genuine. Students respect honesty, especially those who come from at-risk environments or who are marginalized. By being genuine, you not only earn their respect, you also alleviate potential stressors that can occur just from not being genuine with yourself. Let's face it, teaching in higher education is not for the timid. We can be tactful or creative when we express our disappointment in someone for not giving their best, or we can be ecstatic when student group presentations go exceptionally well, just as long as it's genuine.

CHAPTER 7

Moving Beyond Access

Cultivating College Skills and Persistence for Latinx Students

Victoria Christine Rodriguez

> We just have to convince other people that they have power. This is what they can do by participating to make change, not only in their community, but many times changing in their own lives. Once they participate, they get their sense of power.
>
> —Dolores Huerta (Mead, 2016)

INTRODUCTION

For as long as I can remember, my mother made it very clear that I would be attending college one day. She also made it clear that because we did not have a lot of money, I would need to get really good grades in order to attend. And that because I would be the first in my family to complete college, I would need to be willing to ask for help and resources along the way from people outside of my family. A college degree was advertised to me as my ticket out of poverty and into a career that I was passionate about, not just a job to pay the bills. I was fortunate enough to receive a scholarship to a private, college-preparatory high school, where I was able to gain access to some of the resources I needed in order to prepare for and apply to college.

However, in addition to this, my experience there unveiled some educational inequalities. I would compare my experiences in school with those of my neighborhood friends who were attending the local predominantly Latinx, low-income public high school and would notice important differences. My teachers took for granted that we would all be attending college, while my neighborhood friends did not always receive those messages. I had access to a rigorous curriculum without being enrolled in honors or AP courses. My school had a college counselor who met with us individually at least once a year about our pathway to college. My peers from my neighborhood did not have these resources. I felt as though I was an outside observer to both of these worlds, and the disparities in education that I noticed upset me. These experiences sparked my interest in education, and later educational psychology, and propelled me toward a career where I would get to work on this problem of addressing educational inequities.

It still feels strange to introduce myself as "doctor" or "professor." One day as I was walking to the on-campus coffee shop, a student called out to me, "Good morning, Dr. Rodriguez," and I almost completely ignored my student! I didn't realize that the student was referring to me until a few seconds later. When I introduce myself to my students on the first day of classes, I often confess this lingering discomfort and sense of conflict I have about my title. As a Latina first-generation college graduate from a low-income background, using my title can feel at times like "putting on airs." It can make me feel like I am distancing myself from my community. I often fear that people will read or hear my title and perceive me to be positioning myself as better than or above them. However, at the same time, I recognize what an accomplishment my degrees are, not just for myself but also for my community as a whole. My degrees are not my own, but belong to all those who supported me or paved the way for me on my journey. My mother refers to me as "Dr. Mija" (*mija* is "daughter" in Spanish), which for me embodies the balance I search for. She is acknowledging my accomplishments, while at the same time rooting me in my community and acknowledging the other identities I have that I hold dear.

I start with these personal stories because they highlight some of the themes I have heard over the course of my academic career from students, both in K–12 and in higher education, as well as in the research literature. I hope that they also provide readers with some new insight into the foundation for my perspectives as a scholar. My research interests mostly involve looking at the factors that contribute to Latinx students' college readiness and persistence, and how schools can best support underrepresented students throughout this process. This chapter will start by providing some context regarding the state of Latinx education in the country right now. Then I will present an overview of a series of studies I conducted with a predominantly Latinx-serving charter high school regarding the students' and alumni's experiences preparing for and attending college. Here I also will describe some of my findings regarding school practices that supported students as well as some missed opportunities. Next I will offer some reflections on my experiences as a professor and share some techniques I have acquired and implemented in order to support students. My hope for this chapter is that it will increase readers' understanding of what students may have experienced or may be experiencing on their journeys to a college degree, and that educators will feel a sense of agency and urgency to positively contribute to their students' college experiences.

BACKGROUND—THE ASPIRATION-ATTAINMENT GAP

The high school dropout rate for Latinx students has fallen from 34.5% to 9.9% since 1996, and college enrollment rates have seen unprecedented gains, with 35% of college-age Latinxs enrolling in college, but degree attainment rates still lag (Krogstad, 2016). While other gaps in achievement are being chipped away, however slowly, degree attainment rates for Latinx adults have remained consistent since 1995. The percentage of Latinx adults over the age of 25 with an associate's degree was 22.7% and with a bachelor's degree, 15.5%; 42.8% of white adults over 25 held an associate's degree and 32.8% held a bachelor's degree (NCES, 2018a). This gap is referred to as the aspiration–attainment gap. As more and more students aspire to attain a postsecondary degree, we have seen college enrollment rates increase. However, despite this increase in enrollment, we are not observing similar increases in degree attainment for students of color, with Latinx students showing the largest gap in 2-year degree attainment.

Similar gaps have been observed for low-, middle-, and high-income students and have remained consistent since 1990 (NCES, 2018a). The college enrollment rate for high school graduates (including GED recipients) who enrolled immediately after high school was 81% for high-income students, 64% for middle-income students, and 52% for low-income students. In 2002, the Education Longitudinal Study drew from a nationally representative sample of high school sophomores; the students were followed until 8 years after high school graduation. Of the students who graduated from high school and continued on to college, bachelor's degree attainment rates followed a stratified pattern similar to that of enrollment rates. Within 8 years of graduating from high school, 60% of high-income students, 29% of middle-income students, and 14% of low-income students had attained a bachelor's degree (NCES, 2018a). It has long been known that racial and ethnic minorities are overrepresented in low-income brackets, and this is still the case today (Meade, 2014). Therefore, low-income students of color, particularly low-income Latinx students, are the group for whom this aspiration–attainment gap is very pronounced.

CHARTERS AND SCHOOL-LEVEL AND POLICY INTERVENTIONS

Several school-level and policy interventions have been introduced to try to address these gaps in college degree attainment. One is reflected in Obama's 2009 call for schools to prepare students for college and career, and later in the Common Core's college- and career-readiness standards (Allensworth, Nomi, Montgomery, & Lee, 2009; An, 2013). Another is the creation and growing proliferation of charter schools with the mission of "college for all."

Public charter school (PCS) students are more likely to be Latinx and located in a city. Also, they are more likely to attend a high-poverty, racially isolated school compared with traditional public school (TPS) students (National Alliance for Public Charter Schools [NAPCS], 2012; NCES, 2018b). Hill (2008) found that an increasing number of PCSs were adopting college-going missions for their students and providing students with access to a college-preparatory curriculum. For example, KIPP, one of the largest charter networks in the country, states that their mission is: "To create a respected, influential, and national network of public schools that are successful in helping students from educationally underserved communities develop the knowledge, skills, character, and habits needed to succeed in college and the competitive world beyond" (www.kipp.org/kipp-foundation/).

Despite the promise that charter schools represent for some, reports on their effectiveness have been mixed since their inception (Hubbard & Kulkarni, 2009). Various studies of charter schools' effect on student achievement scores have produced mixed results, with some studies showing charter schools to be no different or at times worse than their traditional counterparts (Carnoy, Jacobsen, Mishel, & Rothstein, 2005; Center for Research on Education Outcomes [CREDO], 2009, 2015; Zimmer, Gill, Booker, Lavertu, & Witte, 2012). Charter schools

4-year university but dropped out or later transferred to a community college. This is where I came in. Together with the college counselor, I created a survey for the alumni of the school to find out what higher ed pathways students had chosen after high school. At this point in the history of the school, which had small class sizes, there had been only three graduating classes. As a result, there were only about 60 alumni of the school, and about half of them responded to the survey. Of those who responded, half were enrolled in a 4-year university and a quarter were enrolled in a community college.

Based on the survey responses received, eight alumni were chosen to be interviewed. These alumni were selected based on the year they graduated, their gender, and the kind of postsecondary institution in which they were (or were not) enrolled. In the interviews, students were asked to describe the successes they'd experienced in higher education as well as the struggles. Both administrators from the school and I wanted to identify whether there were any barriers that students experienced that the school could address. All students, regardless of their current status as enrolled or not, identified many of the barriers to persistence that have already been well-documented in the literature (e.g., Walton & Cohen, 2011). Many of these barriers were beyond the reach of BACHS. However, one theme that emerged from these interviews was that the school had provided access but had not necessarily prepared students for the rigor and challenges of college. One student was quoted as saying, "They successfully prepared us to get to college. As they [BACHS] grow, they should prepare the students to stay in college. To deal with actual college obstacles." Students felt as though their school had provided so many supports that once they arrived at college and those supports were removed, they floundered a bit. They had been told in high school that they would need to self-advocate, but once they were at college the fear of being judged and uncertainty around whom exactly to seek help from were overwhelming.

IMPOSTER SYNDROME

I felt immense empathy for these students as I was listening to their stories. I myself was experiencing similar feelings of *imposter syndrome* as a graduate student. So many of them felt ashamed for needing help or guilty for feeling unhappy in school when so many of them had worked so hard to get to that point. These feelings resonated with me. It is a hard position to be in, especially as an 18-year-old living away from family for the first time. As a first-generation college Latina, I felt like my successes were not only mine but my community's. Likewise, my failures were letdowns not only to me but to my community. That carries an immense pressure. You are not only the first in your family trying to pave a way for future generations, but also a representative of an underrepresented and marginalized ethnic group on a college campus. So even though you are told that asking for help is not a sign of weakness and you believe that with your rational mind, if you feel that imposter syndrome, you cannot help but question your sense of belonging when it seems like no one else needs the kind of help you do.

After hearing these stories of both challenges and triumphs, I wanted to spend more time at the school to see how it was preparing students to enter into the world of college and what more it could do. In part, I wanted to investigate whether the school was providing a strong academic foundation so that once students arrived in college they at least would be academically prepared and would not be struggling too severely academically while they were encountering these nonacademic challenges.

I spent the 2015–2016 school year at the high school. I tried to embed myself in and make myself a part of the school environment. I attended classes during the school day; went to parent workshops on college; mentored two seniors through the senior mentor workshops; interviewed students, teachers, and administrators; and finally, attended graduation. I entered into that year wanting to know about the college-readiness process for this particular subpopulation of students at this particular kind of "college for all" charter school. My three guiding research questions were: (1) How are people within the school defining college readiness? (2) What practices within the school do teachers utilize in order to get students ready for college? and (3) What does the college-readiness process look like for first-generation college-going Latinx students a "college for all" charter school? It should be noted that these three research questions don't really address the primary criticism that came from students, which was that the school prepares students to get into college but the academics don't prepare them for college success once they are there.

What Readiness Looks Like

Students, teachers, and administrators all had different definitions for college readiness. When students were asked to describe what it meant to be college ready, they referred to the need to be in the right mindset. Qualities like responsibility and maturity often were cited. Students explained that they needed to develop certain skills, like time management and the ability to self-advocate or reach out for help when necessary. At the same time, students described college as a place where you might not have others to depend on or support you, so it was also necessary to be able to take care of yourself. Teachers' responses included academic preparation, like being able to write a paper. However, teachers' responses also reflected aspects of the students' responses. Teachers cited qualities like maturity, and skills like time management, and explained that being able to write a paper might not matter if the student wasn't also able to be responsible, mature, and able to communicate with professors. Administrators described college readiness in terms of student metrics. In order for students to be college ready, they must complete the A-G curriculum requirements, successfully complete the ACT or SAT, and maintain high GPAs. However, administrators, similar to teachers, also stressed the importance of mindsets and skills, and that these metrics might not accurately describe a student's readiness because they ignore aspects of readiness such as mindsets and skills. The charter network regional office also was asked to provide the network's definition of college readiness and reported that the network simply relied on the metrics described by administrators to define and measure college readiness. The charter network's definition of college readiness had the greatest influence over the structures in place at the school to foster college readiness. These structures focused mostly on fulfilling metrics and less on developing the mindsets and skills everyone else had identified as being foundational to college readiness.

Obstacles to Readiness Preparation

Another key finding from my study was that there were a lot of missed opportunities in the classroom that were hindering students' college-readiness processes. For example, like other charter schools, this one had a high teacher turnover rate and a rather inexperienced faculty. Many teachers struggled to simply maintain order in the classroom because they were still developing their own classroom management styles. This led to frustration not only on the part of the teacher, but also for students. Students expressed frustration and found it unjust that they were not being academically prepared simply because of the rowdiness of a handful of other students in the classroom. Teachers also relied heavily on teacher-centered methods of instruction. While these methods are at times necessary and effective, they have been shown to hinder the development of critical thinking skills and self-monitoring, both important for college readiness, when relied on too heavily in the classroom. Similarly, teachers tended to overscaffold students' experiences in the classroom. For example, note-taking frames were provided to students in classes. Teachers also would specify what parts of the lecture or demonstration should be recorded in students' notes. While this might be an important and necessary thing to do for first-year students and sophomore students as they develop their note-taking skills, there was no gradual reduction in these supports. Even students in their last 2 years in the school were given these supports and were not allowed to practice taking notes on their own. This created a sense of dependence on these supports and communicated a lack of teachers' trust in students' ability to successfully perform these tasks on their own. Simply put, students were not experiencing the preparation and level of academic rigor necessary to be ready for college, and everyone—students, teachers, and administrators—was aware of this fact.

TEACHING UNDERGRADUATE STUDENTS

In the short amount of time that I have been teaching, through graduate school and now as a postdoctoral fellow, I have noticed that students are often hungry to have conversations related to race and racial disparities seen in the United States. This is true not only for students from underrepresented racial or ethnic backgrounds, but also for White students in my classes. Many White students are unsure of how to talk about race and what to do in order to address some of the racial or ethnic inequalities that they've noticed, and are afraid to ask about it. In one of the classes I teach, Understanding Racial and Ethnic Identity Development, we begin the class with discussions regarding the definitions of race, ethnicity, culture, prejudice, and racism, and what the differences are between those terms. We start by operationalizing the terms we're going to be using throughout the semester so that we can all have a similar foundation for discussion and minimize the chance for misunderstanding. Really examining what these different words mean also leads to interesting and fruitful discussion regarding the social construction of concepts like race and ethnicity and how they've been used to perpetuate racial hierarchies throughout history and in the United States. I have seen how these conversations can be enlightening for White students and affirming for students of color. These conversations open up space for students of color to share their own experiences and have those experiences be honored and acknowledged. The students of color that have taken my classes have described to me how reading articles on racial or ethnic inequities in education resonates with their own experiences and affirms what they have been going through. It serves as a way for students to see that they are not alone in their experiences and that people are working to try to address these inequities.

In order to have conversations on race and societal inequities, we do a lot of work at the beginning of the semester to create a positive classroom environment where these conversations can be had. On the first day of class, I have students introduce themselves by sharing four of the most important aspects of their identity, whatever they might be. I also introduce myself in this way. For example, I often describe how being a Latina scholar, a daughter, a ballet folklórico dancer, and a baker are all important parts of my identity. I ask students to describe how these different parts of themselves do or do not intersect as well. So, for me, all of my identities intersect somehow, and I explain these intersections to my students. This aspect of the activity gets them ready for later discussion regarding intersectionality and how it's impossible to look at social identities like "race" or "gender" in isolation or separate from other identities. Also, having students share something deeper about themselves—beyond the standard introductions of name, year in school, and hometown—humanizes them for everyone else. I tell my students that we're going to discuss some heavy topics and that those types of conversations usually are more easily had with friends. We start from a place of trying to develop friendships. We also spend some time setting ground rules for ourselves. I ask students to split up into small groups and come up with rules for discussion for the class. Then we come back together to talk about the rules we've created and decide which ones we will observe for the rest of the semester. These rules are then placed in the course syllabus. In those first days, I also let students know what my expectations of them will be for the semester so that there is no confusion later. Likewise, I ask students to anonymously write down their expectations of me as their teacher. This gives students a voice and an opportunity to let me know what they need from me in order to be successful.

FIVE STRATEGIES

There are five strategies that I use in my classes throughout the semester not only to help students feel comfortable speaking about sometimes uncomfortable topics, but also to set them up for success in my class.

Foster a Sense of Belonging. First, I foster a sense of belonging by communicating that everyone has something to contribute. Everyone's experiences and thoughts are valid as long as they do not intentionally hurt others and can be supported with evidence.

Equalize Participation. Second, I equalize participation. Not all students like participating in large-group discussions. I was one of those students myself. But this does not mean that those students are not participating or engaged. I incorporate multiple avenues for students' participation. These can take the form of online discussion boards, small-group discussions, or personal written reflections at the end of class.

Assignments That Matter. The third practice is that I give assignments that matter. Creating assignments that are more than just busy work has been a goal of mine since I began teaching. I want to create assignments that will be meaningful for students. These can take various forms. For example, one assignment asks students to reflect and write about what they know regarding race, and then to reflect at the end of the semester on what they've learned since. Other assignments attempt to get students to apply what they are learning in the classroom to real-world experiences or problems. Therefore, many of my classes have had a community-engaged learning component. Having assignments that matter helps students to be intrinsically motivated to complete those assignments and see the value in trying to do them well.

Practice Humility. The fourth strategy is that I practice humility. As a teacher, I recognize that I do not and cannot know everything about a topic. Therefore, I balance asserting my authority as an expert in the classroom (being a young, female, Latina scholar) with a sense of humility. I acknowledge that while I can know the literature on racial inequalities in schools, I cannot fully understand the experience of an African American girl, White male, or Latinx boy in school because those are not my social identities or realities.

Recognize That Life Happens. The fifth and final practice is that I recognize that life happens. Students, especially students from under-represented backgrounds, face challenges in their lives too. They have to work, family members die, relationships dissolve, bad days happen. Being empathetic and understanding of this truth can communicate to students authentic care on your part. Instead of thinking that a student is simply lying to get out of class or taking a test, try to give students the benefit of the doubt. I've seen many professors think that a student is lying about whatever excuse the student has given for missing class. While they might have good reason for this—perhaps they've been burned once before—imagine being the student in this situation. How horrible to not have your teacher believe that your grandmother actually died.

These are suggestions I offer not just for helping students of color or other underrepresented students in your classes, but for creating a positive environment in college classes overall.

CHAPTER 8

Supporting the Success of Multilingual Students

Luz Navarette García

> Language is at the center of human life . . . through language we plan our lives and remember our past; we exchange ideas and experiences; we form our social and individual identities. Language is the most unique thing about human beings.
>
> —Cook (2008, p. 1)

AN INTRODUCTION TO THE POWER OF LANGUAGE

The importance of language cannot be overstated. The ability to express, communicate, and comprehend thoughts, feelings, and experiences is inextricably linked to the abilities to create, use, and manipulate language. In addition to the power of language is the power of voice. "Language is essential to the process of dialogue, to the development of meaning, and to the production of knowledge . . . and constitutes a major cornerstone for the development of voice" (Darder, 1997, p. 333). Language is one of our most essential human characteristics and resources.

In a predominantly monolingual country, there is varied acceptance of languages other than English. Other languages are often limited to the peripheries of society, and nondominant languages, voices, and the people associated with them are rarely accepted or treated equitably.

Funds of Knowledge

As has been emphasized over and over in earlier chapters, rather than view our students through a lens of deficit thinking—an overemphasis on the weaknesses or limitations that learners may struggle with—we should begin by reframing this negative perspective. First, educators need to recognize the funds of knowledge (Gonzalez, Moll, & Amanti, 2005) that all students bring from their families, culture, and lived experience. For our multilingual students, their funds of knowledge typically include many years of living beyond the borders of the United States, an international perspective of U.S. history and culture, and knowledge of at least two languages.

Linguistic Discrimination

It is not difficult to find people who espouse the belief that in the United States, English should be not only the official language, but the only language used. The English-only movement is merely an extension of the longstanding discrimination against speakers of world languages. Language variety and dominance in a language other than English, rather than being seen as a benefit, advantage, or fund of knowledge, often is seen as an individual failure on the part of the learner, a systemic failure in the education system, and even a threat to American society (MacDonald & Carrillo, 2006). The suppression of and prejudice against all languages other than English are nothing more than another form of discrimination: "linguistic discrimination" (Attinasi, 1997). Linguistic discrimination includes negative attitudes toward languages, and speakers of languages, other than English, including speakers of English with a non-native accent. This discrimination can lead to societal, personal, and psychological (internal) conflicts, as well as impact the access to and acquisition of English (Attinasi, 1997).

Linguistic Empowerment

> If only you knew me in my native language. Then you'd know how smart I am!
>
> —Anonymous student

The direct opposite of linguistic discrimination is linguistic empowerment. This is when we openly value linguistic and cultural diversity and funds of knowledge that multilingual individuals possess (Lucas, Henze, & Donato, 1990). Rather than look at non-native English-speaking students as having a liability or an insurmountable problem, we must learn to regard languages as resources, as invaluable intellectual capital, and as doorways to opportunities and success (Gándara & Contreras, 2009). It is crucial to acknowledge that solely because a student is not fluent in English does not mean that the individual is not knowledgeable, educated, or capable.

As community college educators of diverse students, it is vital for us to keep these concepts in mind. We may hold conscious or subconscious biases that impact our interactions with and expectations of our multilingual students. Community colleges across the country enroll over 6.5 million students, 24% of whom come from an immigrant background and have a native language other than English (Connell, 2008). The population of multilingual learners in California postsecondary education continues to grow, and "the complexities in addressing the needs of the varied groups of ESL [English as a Second Language] learners must be better understood . . . [and] all faculty, staff, administrators . . . can benefit from a greater understanding of ESL learners in colleges and universities" (Academic Senate for California Community Colleges, 2006, p.1). Thus, educating students from diverse linguistic and cultural backgrounds is not a task that can be left solely to the English as a Second Language Department. As community college educators, we cannot hope, assume, or expect that all language development needs will have been met in ESL or developmental English classes before students reach our classroom. We can work to ensure that our students are not discriminated against (by other students or other educators) solely because of their accent or language proficiency.

As of this writing, California community colleges are in the process of changing the way they assess and place students, with the goal of placing more students directly into transferable, college-level courses (Mejia, Rodriguez, & Johnson, 2016). Many students, including non-native speakers of English, who previously would have had years-long pathways to reach transfer-level courses, will now have the opportunity to enroll in such courses much earlier in their college careers. This will be a change for students and educators alike. Students no longer will be required to take semesters of remedial English or math courses before entering college-level courses. As a result of this change, educators should be prepared to appropriately support a wider range of student abilities than ever before.

So, given these projected changes, how can instructors best support the needs of multilingual learners? One salient issue that affects the educational experience of multilingual students is a lack of recognition of the *experience* of becoming multilingual. The complex process of second-, third-, or fourth-language acquisition is influenced by a multitude of factors.

As you consider how best to support language learners in your current or future classes, begin by imagining yourself in a similar situation. Have you had the experience of studying college-level academic subjects in a foreign language? Would you be able to take your class completely in a foreign language, without textbooks or native language support? What would you need to be successful? How could your professors help you? What support would be most beneficial? What would be most frustrating? What would this experience be like? This is the position that many of our students find themselves in, without the confidence or linguistic knowledge to convey what they need. Also consider that you likely have much more experience and metacognitive awareness as a learner than our students do, especially given that some are in the initial stages of their journeys in higher education.

Thus, the purpose of this chapter is to provide community college instructors with a foundational understanding of the experiences of multilingual learners in their classes. At the very least, this information can help provide awareness and opportunities for collaboration among colleagues who previously haven't considered the significance of this topic. First, I present an overview of who multilingual learners are, so that we can better understand the diverse backgrounds of ESL students. This is followed by an introduction to foundational language-learning theories and specific suggestions for better supporting English learners that, if implemented, will benefit all students.

Who Are Multilingual Learners?

Non-native speakers of English are identified (and self-identify) using a variety of terms. Over the years, the K–12 system in California has transitioned from LEP (limited English proficient) to English language learner (ELL) or English learner (EL). In higher education, ESL is most prevalent and widely used; however, it is important to recognize that many ESL students are learning English as a third or fourth language, and thus the emergence of multilingual learner and other similar terms. For the purposes of this chapter, the terms *multilingual learner*, *EL*, and *ESL student* will be used interchangeably to refer to non-native speakers of English.

The needs of multilingual students are distinct from those of their monolingual peers, yet it is crucial to recognize that even among multilingual learners there is great diversity. Some ELs are new to the United States and, depending on their country of origin, may have taken years of English as a foreign language (EFL), or none at all. Many newcomers, whether immigrants, refugees, or international students, experience various stages of culture shock and trauma, in addition to issues related to language development. Students who are highly educated in their native countries may have vastly different educational philosophies, study habits, and expectations. For long-term California residents, fluency in conversational or communicative English may disguise the need for academic foundations in English. Regardless of language proficiency, multilingual students may or may not have an accent. In fact, often an accent indicates a later age of initial language acquisition, not proficiency.

Furthermore, some multilingual students may not feel that they need additional language development, although they may have been identified as long-term English learners in the K–12 system even upon high school graduation. These students commonly are referred to as Generation 1.5, since they have traits of both first- and second-generation immigrants, although they may have been born in the United States (Rumbaut & Ima, 1988). ESL students may or may not have F-1 (international student) visas. They may or may not be citizens of the United States. They may or may not plan to return to their native country. And just like all members of our diverse community college student population, multilingual students may have stressors we cannot imagine—including working one or more full-time jobs, small children at home, plans to transfer to a university, fears of deportation, or socioeconomic struggles, including housing and/or food insecurity; or they might be wealthy, full-time students with a familial expectation of earning straight As.

Many well-educated international students face challenges acclimating to American-style classrooms due to their different cultural beliefs and traditional educational background. There are two significant issues: (1) years of instruction in EFL by non-native teachers of varying proficiencies who focus on test-taking and the translation of grammar rather than communicative competence, and (2) discomfort with and confusion about U.S. educational expectations and cultural norms (Rhodes, 2017). Often international students have been successful on English tests in their native countries, but that does not necessarily prepare them for the pace of academic instruction or meaningful communication in English. They have studied textbook English, but have not been expected to think critically or communicate effectively in English, and rarely with native speakers of English. This experience is extremely frustrating for students who feel an inordinate amount of pressure and whose families are investing international student tuition expecting that their children will be academically successful.

Whether we get to know our students well enough to learn their backgrounds and stories is up to each of us, but we cannot ignore the reality that, with ever-changing demographics and the diverse linguistic needs of students, community college educators need to be better equipped to understand and support multilingual learners.

A CRASH COURSE IN LANGUAGE DEVELOPMENT THEORIES

The length of time it takes to learn a new language varies greatly. "While conversational verbal proficiency can be developed within a couple of years, it takes, for most non-native English speakers, five to seven [some studies indicate 10] years under optimal conditions to achieve the level of academic language skills necessary" Suárez-Orozco, Suárez-Orozco, & Todorova, 2010, p. 42) to compete academically. Note that the time estimate of 5 to 7 years is under optimal conditions.

There are many factors that impact language development. These factors include access, use, and value of the second language (L2); methods of instruction; and learner characteristics such as language aptitude, personality, academic preparation, urgency, motivation, and even age. In terms of the impact of age on language learning, "older means faster in terms of rate of acquisition of morphology and syntax, while younger is better in terms of final level of attainment of accent-free, nativelike proficiency" (Valdés, 2001, p. 20). A critical- or sensitive-period hypothesis has not been proven other than for phonology (pronunciation). Young children learning a new language have a more basic level of language to learn to reach grade level, they have more time, and they are more often able to acquire native-like pronunciation. Adults have more cognitive maturity and are more aware of the learning process. Still, children and adults go through similar stages in second-language acquisition (Krashen, 1982; Valdés, 2001).

There are two fundamental language development theories that are essential to understand when preparing to support the needs of multilingual students: Vygotsky's zone of proximal development and, although thoroughly debated, Krashen's five hypotheses.

Vygotsky's Zone of Proximal Development

The ZPD, as discussed earlier, is the sweet spot for learning. It encompasses the skills that are within proximity of a learner's current language level. If a target skill is too far beyond the learner's current level of mastery, it is nearly impossible for the student to reach it without appropriate guidance, contextualization, or support.

It is incumbent on the instructor to provide levels of scaffolding until the learner can reach the target with minimal support. The ZPD underscores the need for understanding student levels and abilities so as to provide instruction that is within an appropriate zone to allow for growth.

Krashen's Five Hypotheses

Few theories in second-language acquisition have had as much influence or engendered as much controversy as Krashen's (1982) five hypotheses: the acquisition-learning hypothesis, the natural order hypothesis, the monitor hypothesis, the input hypothesis, and the affective filter hypothesis. Although each of these hypotheses continues to be debated and refined (Romeo, 2000), it is useful to understand them. In the *acquisition-learning hypothesis*, a distinction is made between acquiring a language naturally and learning it in an educational setting.

A natural approach is preferred over a rigid classroom approach, as indicated by how children acquire language naturally: immersion and real-life communicative needs. The *natural order hypothesis* builds on the idea of the acquisition-learning hypothesis and recognizes that there are some grammatical structures that seem to be acquired prior to others. Rather than teach this explicitly, it is helpful to recognize that there is an order in natural language acquisition, and that students will learn at their own pace. The *monitor hypothesis* is the concept that language learners who have formally studied a language develop an internal monitor: a critical editor that regulates how comfortable they are taking risks and producing the new language. The internal language monitor may be stronger and more prohibitive in introverts, who prefer more time to think and edit before producing language that may not be grammatically accurate.

Krashen's final two hypotheses are the most relevant to language educators and general educators alike: the input hypothesis and the affective filter hypothesis. The *input hypothesis* is very closely related to Vygotsky's zone of proximal development. Similarly, it posits that language learners must have comprehensible input in order to grow. They must be able to understand some of the content in order to begin to understand more. Much like Vygotsky's ZPD suggests scaffolding to reach new levels, the input hypothesis indicates that input should be just one level above the student's current level. This is ideally more challenging than what the student already knows, but not so challenging that the learner is overwhelmed. Finally, Krashen's *affective filter hypothesis* reminds us that language acquisition is influenced by affective factors such as motivation, anxiety, confidence, and self-esteem. When a student's anxiety and self-esteem are raised, a mental block is formed. It is helpful for educators to find ways to lower a student's affective filter, which allows more learning to take place by minimizing the mental block.

NINE SUGGESTIONS TO SUPPORT MULTILINGUAL LEARNERS

1. *Learn as much as you can about your students.* What are their educational and linguistic backgrounds? What are their goals? Even if you have large lecture classes, this information can be gathered through a brief informational survey given to all students at the beginning of each semester, or less systematically during office hours.

2. *Be aware of and challenge your assumptions.* Better yet, don't make assumptions! If a student has an accent, that doesn't mean the student is less intelligent, underprepared, or unable to understand you. Don't assume that all students share understanding of cultural references or idiomatic expressions.

3. *Envision and communicate high expectations and limitless opportunities for all students.* Sometimes students are limited by others' stereotypes, and sometimes the limitations are self-imposed. Individual educators have the power (and the duty) not only to recognize student potential, but to cultivate it.

4. *Recognize and foster a variety of forms of knowledge and expertise among students.* Many students have life experiences, skills, and perspectives (funds of knowledge) that can enrich our classes. Some multilingual students have undergraduate or graduate degrees in their native countries. They may be professionals who are working to improve English skills in their field. We must work diligently to provide safe spaces that recognize and value student identities and backgrounds, without practicing or allowing others to practice linguistic (or any other form of) discrimination. Students need to know they belong and are loved. Don't we all?

5. ***Provide ample wait time.*** Thinking and learning in a new language are extremely cognitively demanding. They are taxing and exhausting, and multilingual students may expend more mental energy than native English speakers when given the same task. Students need time to process, think, reflect, and respond. Some students translate using a cell phone or other device, and some translate mentally. More proficient students do not need to translate, but they still need extra time to process. When asking a question in class, do not call on students who raise their hands before you even finish asking the question. Ask the question, then give all students time to "think before they speak." This may mean giving them time to write their thoughts. Another strategy is "think-pair-share." This allows students time to think and share their thoughts with a partner. These strategies encourage more participation than simply calling on one student for an answer, which gives all the other students reprieve from engaging in the process. You also can let a student know ahead of time that you are going to ask that student to answer a question. This allows the student to carefully prepare while still demonstrating and sharing knowledge with others.

6. ***Connect your students with campus resources.*** Talk about the importance of meeting with a counselor. Make sure students know that the best and most successful students meet with tutors, visit during office hours, and make use of the resources available. They may be under the impression that seeking help is a sign of weakness; help to dispel that notion. Explain the concept of office hours and encourage/invite/require students to participate in your office hours as you see fit.

7. ***Contextualize your content as much as possible.*** Provide meaningful visuals. Be sure that all instructions are clear and in writing. Avoid relying solely on verbal instructions or cues. Speak naturally and clearly.

8. ***Distinguish between different language skills. Language skills include listening, speaking, reading, writing, and critical thinking.*** Learners do not develop all of these domains equally. Receptive skills (the ability to understand input by reading or listening) are usually more developed than expressive skills (the ability to produce and express language through writing or speaking). This explains why a student may be able to read the textbook or understand the lecture, but still experience difficulty with production (written or oral).

9. ***Avoid asking questions that students cannot answer.*** Do not ask, "Do you understand?" or "Any questions?" Even, "What are your

questions?" is flawed. Rather, find ways to check for understanding that truly foster student thinking and reflection. Ask students to reiterate instructions to one another or to you. Ask students to explain their first step, next step, and so on. Ask students to hand you one question written on a Post-it as they walk out the door.

This chapter explores the power of language, the importance of recognizing and deploying funds of knowledge, as well as raising awareness of linguistic discrimination. Linguistic empowerment underscores the importance of reframing deficit thinking and consciously adopting a more comprehensive and empowering perspective. This glimpse into the lives of multilingual learners helps community college educators begin to explore and understand the diverse backgrounds of ESL students, especially given current trends and changes in policy and legislation to allow more access to college-level classes. Vygotsky's and Krashen's foundational language-learning theories provide helpful insight into the importance of knowing where students are in order to help them grow, and the significance of affective variables such as motivation and self-esteem. Finally, the implementation of the nine suggestions above will benefit all students, especially language learners.

In conclusion, given the increasing diversity of student backgrounds, needs, and skill levels, community college educators must consciously learn and implement new strategies that address the specific academic needs and educational concerns of our multilingual students. Often, what we do to support our multilingual students will have a positive impact on all students. In addition to exploring and considering the nine recommendations set forth in this chapter, community college educators should begin this dialogue with colleagues, administrators, and multilingual students on campus. Educators also should consider taking part in ongoing professional development opportunities and identifying or creating content-specific resources to better serve the needs of multilingual learners in their discipline. This dialogue also can continue in professional organizations across the disciplines; it is not a topic that can be left solely to English as a Second Language instructors.

CHAPTER 9

Teaching College and Career Skills in Ways That Dignify Students

> Students who are academically underprepared do twice the work as academically prepared students during a course, because they are mastering academic skills while simultaneously mastering the course content.

To teach college and career skills in ways that dignify students' lived experiences, instructors can draw from topics in previous chapters. These include using inquiry-based, interactive learning; developing strong communities of learners; fostering a growth mindset classroom; and framing instructional practices in terms of an equity mindset. This chapter offers strategies to bolster the college and career skills of students with learning disabilities and to support students experiencing anxiety and trauma.

BOLSTERING COLLEGE AND CAREER SKILLS

Teaching college skills is an equity issue. Every student deserves equal access to instruction of the content. If some students do not have access because they lack specific academic skills, then that is unfair. Explicitly teaching college and career skills can break down barriers for these students and ultimately improve their chances of attaining 4-year degrees. Examples of college skills are: knowing how to study for a test; deciphering assignment directions; knowing how to take notes; using academic language; writing an essay; and knowing how to communicate with a professor. Instructor Regina Guerra gives an example of a simple college skill: "For the first homework assignment, I write 'p. 237, #s 45–89' on the board. Some students only complete number 45 and 89, because they think it signifies to only complete those two problems. We have to teach students what this means without embarrassing them." Career skills are skills that help students be successful in the 21st-century workplace. The National Education Association's four Cs of career readiness are critical thinking, communication, collaboration, and creativity and innovation. Some examples of career skills are: working in teams; writing professional academic emails; communicating students' unique approaches to problem solving; doing a job interview; managing time; and presenting orally.

A history instructor teaches a class of 35 students and only 16 students finish, but they get As and Bs. What happened? The 19 students who needed extra support dropped out. The 16 remaining were students with stronger academic skills, who did not need support. When teaching first-year college students in developmental classes, instructors commonly see many students struggle to maintain a C average during the entire semester. It takes a lot of hard work to keep retention rates as high as possible and to fight for every single student. It is not equitable to lose the 50% of students in our classes who have fewer college skills and more gaps in knowledge. It is not equitable to deliver instruction that meets the needs of only the 50% of students who are already prepared.

To make instruction equitable, we need to spiral in enough college skills to retain students who require extra support. However, we need to do it in ways that leave students with their dignity intact. Here is an example of spiraling in, or layering in, the teaching of college skills. During class, an instructor shows an instructional video on the anatomy of the human hand, Nat Turner's rebellion, how to perform CPR, how to dissect an article, or how to solve an equation. This may provide another instructor's perspective and also deepen content knowledge. After the video, the instructor spirals in the teaching of college skills. She says, "You can find a lot of videos like this on the Internet by googling. Before you come to class, you can watch a video to pre-learn material." I give students the example of Marla Carrington from Chapter 4, who pre-learned the material before math class and went from a C- to an A. This is an example of layering in college skills. Instructors can take a regular strategy of showing the content using instructional videos and turn it into an opportunity to teach the college skills of locating and using resources to advance personal growth and professional advancement.

Teaching college skills is not about watering down the curriculum. I tell first-year students, "If your first year feels hard, it is because it *is* hard. You are doing twice the work of students who are in their second year. You are learning how to succeed in college while simultaneously mastering course content. The good news is that this gets better with time and by your second year, college will be a lot easier." Similarly, instructors who layer in college skills while simultaneously teaching the course content are also doing twice the work of instructors who focus solely on teaching content to the already academically prepared students. The following are 20 strategies that instructors can layer into asset-based classroom instruction to teach college skills.

Strategy 1: Praise Skills and Not Ability

Spend instructional minutes praising students' academic skills. Because the instructional approach and strategies advocated within these pages involve a lot of group-work and small- and large-group discussions, evidence of student learning is made explicit through conversations. Therefore, there are ample opportunities to pepper instruction with growth mindset praise and feedback around college skill development. Instructors can tell students:

"You have strong skills at diagnosing what you do not know."

"Clearly, you work hard on studying."

"Thank you for asking really hard questions. It slows the class down and gives everyone the opportunity to deepen their conceptual knowledge."

Instructors can give praise to individuals or the entire class.

"This class has great adaptive skills."

"This class has great study skills."

"You are competent math learners."

"I believe that in your next math class, you will figure out which study skills you will need to learn in order to excel."

Giving a lot of feedback around skills and the learning process helps to foster a growth mindset classroom. After an instructor has affirmed students' skills and emphasized the process 20 times in a class, still a student might ask, "We are a smart class, right?" It is hard to resist the temptation to say, "Hey, you are smart." It is important to avoid confirming that fixed mindset way of thinking and keep the focus on praising skill development. Instead, an instructor could respond, "Yes, this class has great study skills, you come to class on time, and you ask really good questions. These strategies help you learn math better."

Strategy 2: Model College and Career Skills

Frequently, first-gen students do not possess social capital that guarantees college success, because their parents did not graduate with a 4-year degree. Social capital refers to the accumulation of college and career experience and acumen derived from social networks, to which more-affluent students belong. First-gen students cannot draw from this bank of social connections with people who have the lived experiences of going to college to help guide them through their college journey. The instructor may be the first person with whom they will have an academic conversation. The instructor may be the first person they know who has a master's degree. First-gen students may wonder, "How do I shake hands with a professor? What is considered too long when maintaining eye contact? What does an office visit look like?" Students who have parents with master's and doctoral degrees have been exposed to shaking hands with Dr. Miller and asking Dr. Simpson, "Can I come work part-time in your chiropractic office after school?" They have already socialized with people with advanced degrees.

As instructors of first-gen students, we are always modeling these professional academic skills when we begin class on time, use professional academic language, or wear professional attire. I explain to students that I am not the only professional academic model. I explain, "You may call me Felicia. However, other instructors may want you to address them as 'professor' or 'doctor.'" While we model academic behavior, we also can teach it explicitly. For example, an instructor can discuss the idea of teaching-style compatibility. It is a great college and career skill to understand that instructors, managers, student-peers, and coworkers all have different teaching, management, or work styles, but still operate in a professional academic setting.

Strategy 3: Leverage the Community of Learners

From Day 1 we do group-work and begin co-constructing a community of learners. I leverage these connections to teach study skills and college-success skills. For example, after 3 weeks students discuss the prompt, "Which skills have I improved so far?" Many students mention math skills like "fractions" or "solving equations." However, they also mention soft skills like "communicating in groups," "doing my homework consistent-ly," "asking for help," and "coming to class on time." It is important for students who have been absent to get caught up before they return to class, so I link their behavior to the group's success. I might publicly say, "Lucy, you were absent and I noticed that you got caught up before you came back to class. That helps to keep everyone in class learning at their top levels." Sometimes when a few people have been absent, I do not mention their names, and I remind the class about the coaching and team metaphor. I say, "When you miss a class and do not get caught up before you return, you impact the entire class's learning process for that day. You cannot contribute in groups or in whole-class discussions at a high level, either." I remind students of the online list of resources and activities for getting caught up that our class created collaboratively during the first 2 weeks.

I refer to the team analogy. "Does anyone play on a team? What happens when you play on a team where people are not as conditioned or prepared as you are, or if the coach is super distracted that day?" or, "I play tennis. When I play with someone who is at the top of their game, I play better." Without first building a strong community of learners, I am not sure how well this strategy would work. However, when students feel responsible for one another, they push a little harder. If someone has been absent a couple of times and does not have the work made up before returning, I will send an email along the following lines: "We miss you and I would like to remind you that it affects the class when you come to class unprepared."

Strategy 4: Explicitly Teach Mentoring Skills

First-gen students may not have mastered the process of procuring a mentor yet. Studies suggest that students from low-income households may possess an autonomy that may be at odds with navigating the cul-ture at educational institutions (Darling, 2017, 2019; Lareau, 2003; Rogoff, Paradise, Arauz, Correa-Chávez, & Angelillo, 2003). They may be used to depending on themselves. Students may not understand how to get a mentor or "game the system," as Juan Soto, a first-gen college student, calls it. You may have to explain what mentoring looks like and why it is helpful for students' educational and career goals. In addition, based on past experiences, students of color may not trust that the system will serve them, so making the extra effort to reach out may be necessary.

this cultural pride around their identity, *yet*. One exception is the deaf and hard-of-hearing community, which embraces a cultural identity that communicates pride. In fact, according to Laura, members of that community do not identify as having a disability. Still, there is hope that students with disabilities may one day develop more pride around their identities. For example, a growing grassroots movement exists that celebrates neurodiversity. It argues that neurological differences like ADHD and autism are normal variations in the human genome and should be valued. In addition, Laura talks about how students with autism have exceptional skills in some very specific areas.

Unfortunately, many students with disabilities conceal their disability when they are navigating a system in which they feel like an outsider. First-gen students with disabilities have to navigate the same social system as other first-gen, ethnic/racial minority, low-income, and LGBTQ+ students. They just have to do it while also having a disability. Laura says, "We expect them to do a lot independently." They have to self-identify, seek out services that support them, provide verification of their disability, provide a letter of accommodation to their instructors, and facilitate the process of getting accommodations around testing, assistive devices, special equipment, and so on.

The following are seven of Laura's recommended strategies—and one of mine—for supporting students with disabilities.

Strategy 1: Set the Tone Early

Laura says, "We explicitly teach students to approach instructors and set up a meeting to talk further about their accommodations." I joked, "It is not working." I told her, "During the first week of the semester, students with disabilities furtively hand me their accommodation letters, frequently while I am speaking with another student—and then just sort of vaporize. They try to slip it in under the radar." Laura interjects, "Yes, they are trying to pass." By "pass," she means that they are trying to come off as a student without a disability. How can instructors make sure they are not complicit in this process of shadowing part of these students' identities?

Laura suggests that instructors say, "Thank you so much. I would like to get to know you better. Let's talk during office hours. This is really important information. I want to make sure that you get what you need out of class." Responding in this way validates the student and makes the process of communicating about the disability easier and more transparent. Also, it takes the stigma off having the disability.

Strategy 2: Use "People First" Language

Language is powerful. You may have noticed that in the stereotype exercise in Chapter 3 I purposely did not use "people first" language, because I wanted to generate classic stereotypes. I said, "homeless people" instead of "people who do not have homes." Shifting to "people first" language makes it harder to generalize about groups of people. Laura says, "Saying 'DRD [Disability Resources Department] students' is a bit generalizing or stigmatizing." Instead she says, "students with disabilities," "students with autism," or "students with an intellectual disability." She adds, "Intellectual disability is a designation that includes students with lower IQs and those who experience syndromes such as Down's Syndrome, and was previously referred to as 'developmentally delayed learners.'"

Strategy 3: Question the Balance of the Basis of Grade

In terms of the balance of the basis of grade, Laura recommends spreading the weighting out over several categories. Tests, homework, quizzes, projects, quick-writes, and participation are some typical categories. She recommends avoiding weighting too heavily in one category over another. When she is looking for the best course for students, if testing is weighted heavily and that will be a barrier to success for a student, she steers the student toward a course that has less weight on tests.

Laura adds, "These students have multiple risk factors in addition to a disability. Here we need to focus on intersectionality of the student. They may have a disability. Also, they may be first-gen, an immigrant, African American, Latinx, or a veteran. They may have housing or food insecurity, lived in foster care, or spent time incarcerated. For these students teetering on the edge it is easier to build on success than it is to come back from failure. If a student struggles with a particular area, it gives them air beneath the wings to have some success. We want students to be prepared and encouraged."

Strategy 4: Question Your Assessments

Curriculum should be accessible to all students. Therefore, Laura recommends that we challenge our assumptions around what it means to master the curriculum. She suggests that we ask and keep asking, "What really are we trying to measure with a particular assessment?" Laura recounts a story: She asked an instructor, "Why do you give pop quizzes? What are you hoping to measure?" The instructor responded, "I just want to see where the students are. But how am I going to give extra time [for students with disabilities] for a pop quiz?" Laura responded, "Oh then, they do not need to be graded. If you are giving a pop quiz to hold students accountable, then that is different. It does not have to be timed." I give choices on assessments. I do several ungraded, checking-for-understanding assessments in class like exit tickets, mini-quizzes, mini-presentations—none of them for grades. Sometimes I will differentiate these assessments. For example, I give three problems of increasing complexity for exit tickets. I tell students, "If your skills are at this level right now, then do all three. If they are at this level, then do just the first one. However, you will all have to know the content at this top level before the test." One final suggestion from Laura is to give students options about types of assessments. For example, they can choose a final that is either a project, a paper, or a final exam.

Strategy 5: Learn More About Universal Design

Like other identity groups, students with disabilities are not a monolithic group, so there is great diversity within the group. Therefore, there is no one-size-fits-all instructional approach. **Universal design** provides universal access to all students, but it may especially benefit students with disabilities. Laura elaborates:

> The idea of universal design is to mitigate barriers for students. Also, maybe these instructional approaches help other students, too.
>
> Universal design has its roots in architecture. For example, maybe there is a student who uses a wheelchair. Not just a student in a wheelchair benefits from a curb cut [leveling off the curb] added to the sidewalk. What about the person with a stroller, the person who broke their leg, is carrying a bundle of wood, or is wheeling luggage? So, this curb cut makes the sidewalk universally accessible. It is not just for the student with a disability. You can apply that lens to curriculum. What can I do to make the content more accessible? [The curricular adaptation] is also for the first-generation college student, the English learners—all of those different categories.
>
> When I teach, I try to deliver my material in as many modalities as possible. So maybe I give a lecture. Maybe I post the notes on Canvas for the entire class. Also, I have students rotate as note-takers who take turns using the Live Scribe pen to take notes for the class. Also, the lecture

is being recorded. That way students can look at it again; they can read it again; and they can hear it again. If a student is not comfortable I don't make them [be the note-taker]. However, what's really nice about it is [that] seeing other people take notes normalizes the apprehension around note-taking for students. Note-taking in college is hard and students are freaked out about note-taking. Students have to discern between what is important and not . . . and synthesize the information and decide what is so important at the time. Notes are not a verbatim account of what happens in class. This is universal design. It makes [content] accessible to everyone. However, you can't solve everything. I have students who may never complete their math requirement. That is real. This is the point where the rubber meets the road, but we can do things to mitigate the barriers.

Strategy 6: Invite the Disability Specialist to Class

Have the disability specialist speak to your class. The visit could make you and your students better informed about how to build a community of learners that is inclusive for students with disabilities.

Strategy 7: Communicate Directly to Students

If a student has an aide, interpreter, or note-taker, always address the student with disabilities and not the aide. And never refer to a student with disabilities in the third person in conversation.

Strategy 8: Give More Wait Time

Wait time, covered in Chapter 8, is a great strategy. To illustrate the importance of providing wait time to accommodate students who take longer to process, take these two 10-second quizzes. You will need a pen, paper, and 10 seconds on a timer. For the first quiz, you will use your customary writing hand. Write the answers to the following three questions in 10 seconds:

1. What color is an avocado?
2. What color is a lemon?
3. What color is a car tire?

Okay, now with your non-writing hand, you are going to take another 10-second quiz. Go ahead and put 10 seconds on a timer. Write the answers to the following three questions in 10 seconds:

1. What color is the sky?
2. What color is chocolate?
3. What color is a strawberry?

Did you feel, "I know these answers. I just need more time"?

Some students (e.g., English learners, students with disabilities, students with anxiety) need more time than others to process language and respond. When asking a probing question, give that extra 10–20 seconds to allow more students to process the language. I ask students to remind me to slow down and provide wait time. If one student consistently blurts out answers too fast, I say, "Today, everyone needs to raise their hand and wait to be called on before they respond." Also, it is important to hold students who take a longer time accountable for participation. If I know Adrian needs more time to process a question, I say, "Adrian, I am going to ask you to answer number 7, when we get there."

Students with learning disabilities are not defined by their disability, and do not like to have their disability framed in a deficit manner. Here is one example about framing visual impairments as assets. Using an fMRI, scientists discovered that people who are blind rewire their neural networks in ways that provide them with remarkable auditory perception. Students who are blind can comprehend people speaking at 25 syllables per second—although no one actually can speak that fast (Fields, 2010). In fact, normal conversations are spoken at the rate of six syllables per second. An announcer reading the fine print at the end of an advertisement is talking at about 10 syllables per second.

PROVIDING SUPPORT FOR ANXIETY, STRESS, AND TRAUMA

This section describes ideas for understanding trauma and alleviating anxiety—mostly around test-taking. Students may take these ideas and apply them to alleviating anxiety in other areas of their lives. However, if students are experiencing crippling anxiety from the effects of trauma, then an instructor should refer them to campus resources.

Strategy 1: Create a Safe, Engaging Classroom

Creating a safe, engaging classroom with explicit and consistent norms is the first step in supporting students who have experienced trauma. The preceding chapters discuss research and strategies for creating this safe learning environment where all students are comfortable making mistakes, taking risks, and sharing their unique approaches. Differentiated instruction, carefully scaffolded activities, and instruction framed with an equity mindset contribute to creating a community of learners where students evolve as competent learners.

Strategy 2: Connect Students with Resources

Do more "inreach." Bring in guests or share slides and brochures from the Mental Health Services Department and other programs at your school for supporting students experiencing stress. Also, become familiar with the signs of students' distress and the process for referring students to the intervention team.

Strategy 3: Help Students Overcome Test-Taking Anxiety and Other Anxiety

Most instructors are not counselors, so rather than talk about anxiety around trauma, we may be more comfortable targeting our discussion of anxiety toward alleviating test-taking anxiety. This allows students to explore these anxiety-reducing strategies and decide whether they are relevant to other areas of their lives.

Before the first test, I do a 15-minute session on test-taking anxiety and strategies. I put up a color slide similar to the black and white one in Figure 9.1. It describes the Yerkes-Dodson Law (Yerkes & Dodson, 1908). I tell students, "In order to perform well on tests, students need to have just the right amount of anxiety. If they are experiencing too little or too much anxiety, then they will perform poorly." I illustrate with a story from my own life: "I was a stoner in high school, because my life had fallen apart, and I did not understand any other way to deal with it. I showed up at class stoned for my calculus make-up test, and got 0%. If you are too laid back for a test, then you will do poorly. Similarly, if you are too anxious for a test, then you will do poorly too." I explain, "If I was standing in the middle of the road and a car was coming at me . . . or I was standing in the middle of the Serengeti and a wildebeest was running at me . . . I am here, like a deer in headlights, trying to decide what I should do. Freeze? Run to the left? Run to the right? Scream? How well do you think I would be at doing a math problem at that moment?" Everyone laughs. I continue, "When the brain is faced with a perceived threat, it cannot solve math problems well in that moment."

Figure 9.1. The Sweet Zone for Performance

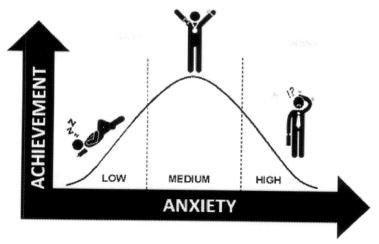

I show a slide where the limbic part of the brain having to do with threats and emotional regulation is lit up. I explain that the frontal lobe is in charge of executive functioning. That is one of the regions of the brain that lights up when we are learning or solving math problems. If the brain is consumed with dealing with a threat, then the frontal lobe functioning gets hijacked. I explain, "Anxiety can be like a whisper. A student, Jarnell, kept telling me he was very anxious about geometry. One day I helped him with a perimeter-of-a-rectangle problem and I asked, 'What is 2 inches plus 4 inches?' He just looked at me blankly for several seconds. I said, 'Are you feeling anxious?' He said, 'No.' Then he said, 'Oh, that is what anxiety feels like.'"

I explain how when students have too little anxiety about a test they perform poorly, and if they have too much anxiety they perform poorly. There is an anxiety "sweet zone" that maximizes performance during testing. Also, I share some strategies. One is called "name it and tame it," coined by Dr. Daniel Siegel. Before a test, I have students hold up fingers in front of their chest so only I can see. "One" is "not anxious at all" and "five" is "too anxious." I also have them do this when we begin a word problem to normalize the idea that even Einstein felt anxious when he started a word problem that was novel to him. (This is a growth mindset move, too, as I am communicating that even experts struggle.) I say, "If you are at a 'five' with anxiety, just by naming that, it will drop to a 'three'—which is perfect for optimizing performance." In the middle of the test, I ask them again about their anxiety, to get them to dial it down.

Strategies students can try *before* the day of the test are: (1) get organized and begin studying on the first day of the unit; (2) synthesize class notes after every session; (3) get every homework question answered during the 3 weeks before the test; (4) over-study for the test the week before the test; (5) during the week before the test, envision being calm when taking the test (use free relaxation tape by Dr. Joe Persinger at www.drjoepersinger.com/downloads/).

Strategies students can try during a test are: (1) use **"name it and tame it"** to dial down anxiety; (2) start with problems or parts that make them feel confident and competent; (3) do **bilateral tapping** with positive affirmations; (4) get physical with **somatic experiencing, movement, and talk;** (5) breathe (do **4-7-8 breathing** and **smiling breathing**); (6) do a **brain dump** at the beginning of the test.

Strategy 4: Leverage Trauma Resources

Therapies that alleviate post-traumatic stress disorder (PTSD) also support student learning. They include eye movement desensitization and reprocessing (EMDR), somatic experiencing trauma therapy (SE), and hypnosis. You may want to invite a trauma expert like Dr. Joe Persinger to present to faculty at your college. Also, you can learn more about trauma and the body and brain from the following books: *Scared Sick: The Role of Childhood Trauma in Childhood Disease* by Robin Karr-Morse and Meredith S. Wiley; *The Body Keeps the Score: Brain, Mind, and Body in the Healing of Trauma* by Bessel van der Kolk; *Waking the Tiger: Healing Trauma* by Peter Levine; *In an Unspoken Voice* by Peter Levine; and *Why Zebras Don't Get Ulcers* by Robert M. Sapolsky.

This chapter discussed strategies for teaching college and career skills in ways that dignify students' lived experiences. Also, it offered strategies to help students with learning disabilities excel. Finally, it touched on alleviating anxiety and working with students who have trauma. To learn more about the activities in bold, go to www.feliciadarling.com.

CHAPTER 10

Beyond the Classroom

One of a community college instructor's most important roles is to breathe life into students' big dreams.

This chapter focuses on the idea of pushing out beyond boundaries in three ways. First, it demonstrates how instructors can move beyond bolstering student success in our classrooms toward supporting students' career and life dreams. Second, it offers ideas for implementing this *Teachin' It!* model of instruction outside of the physical classroom in online and hybrid courses. Finally, the chapter encourages instructors to break out of teaching in silos to maximize our teaching potential through collaboration in communities of practitioners.

TOWARD THE NEXT COURSE, DEGREE, CAREER, LIFE

Instructors can lay the groundwork for student success beyond the classroom and well into students' careers and lives. For example, during a semester, an anatomy instructor: teaches content so that students pass the midterm and final exams; layers in strategies for passing both essay and multiple-choice quizzes; fosters positive academic mindsets; explicitly teaches professional academic behavior; and facilitates the development of students' identities as competent scientists. She teaches everything students need to be successful in the course.

However, as an instructor of first-gen college students, the instructor is the only one in the room with an advanced degree—the only one who knows what happens after this course, and the next course, and the AA, and the bachelor's, and in the career field. If students are not first-generation college students, maybe they already know how to shake an MD's hand, because their mother's best friend is a pediatrician. Maybe they are already committed to the career goal of being a dentist, because their aunt is a dentist. However, for first-gen students, the instructor may be the only person they know who has a career based on an advanced degree. This is especially true if this is their first college course. Therefore, the instructor is uniquely positioned to lay the groundwork for students to envision a path greater than just passing this course—to inspire a vision that casts students' eyes further along the horizon toward a professional career.

To support students' broader visions, instructors should explicitly teach test-taking strategies useful for subsequent courses in the career pathway; reinforce that students will need to continue to refine their study skills to be successful in the next course and the next; and talk about bachelor's and advanced degrees and careers in the field. I invite students to contact me about getting a letter of recommendation for scholarships and jobs. I say, "Think about which strengths you exhibit in class and make sure you mention them in your request for a letter. This puts the idea in their heads that this class is but one step on a longer journey to a degree or a career. Also, I talk about masters degrees and PhDs. Sometimes I have students who persist through the entire semester and still do not pass the course. I send them an email to encourage them to retake the class in order to continue to reach their career goals.

In the following excerpt, Jerry Miller, Senior Dean of Career and Technical Education, talks about how course content we teach every day is transferable to many careers.

> These days, it is not always about your degree or certificate. It can be about a transferable skill set. For example, someone who is interested in robotics may get a job in engineering or they may end up working in Amy's kitchen to oversee the assembly line process. They may be in a winery working in the bottling department. Plus, there are all these crossover business startups in Silicon Valley. Transferable skills may be more important than the exact type of degree. Don't just say, "I will be a realtor." Realtors listen and communicate. Psychology would be great for a safety officer or a police officer. Google hires people who are psychology or philosophy inclined. This is a big shift. [In the past], you applied to do a job that matched with your degree. Now they are asking, During your degree program, What did you study? What knowledge do you have?"

English instructor Ann Foster talks about teaching life skills in courses.

> So, if we think about [literature] we get principles and ethics and codes to live by, ways of living in the world. It offers a glimpse into the world of humanities through fictional characters that can help us determine our

compass. Students ask, "How do I align with these characters? How do they bother me? How do I love them? How can they inform my life?" Someone could argue that literature is as important as composition . . . that it is more important to college and career skills . . . that a person needs to develop a way of living and being in the world.

Graduating student Colin Hargove, in the 2018 SRJC commencement address, underscores how instructors are dream makers who breathe life into students' dreams.

Our time here has literally changed us forever. You encouraged us when we wanted to give up, and you never stopped believing that we could pull it off—even though at times, we [stopped believing]. Thank you for loving and believing in us. Without you, for most of us, none of this would be happening today. We learned to find comfort in the uncomfortable because this is the place where we write better drafts of ourselves. We learned here that failure isn't a character flaw, but rather an opportunity for growth, because falling down is inevitable, but getting up is transcendent.

In this secure harbor that is Santa Rosa Junior College, we have safely learned how to learn. [We appreciate] the professor who found a way to breathe life into our own motivation, passion, and creativity. [Our experiences] have inspired our hearts to surrender to a more wakeful state, leading to a reconditioning of the soul, allowing a more authentic relationship with ourselves and the world that surrounds us.

ONLINE AND HYBRID TEACHING AND LEARNING

This section discusses overarching principles that may help when implementing the *Teachin' It!* model into online instruction. The first step is to foster a growth mindset about your ability to deliver asset-based instruction online. You will get better at it over time, but you will have to solve a lot of problems and challenges, and you will make mistakes as you continue to get better at it. To integrate the same guiding principles of in-person instruction into your online model: (1) implement the social constructivist approach; (2) approach all aspects of online instruction with an equity mindset; (3) develop a strong community of learners with the online tools available; (4) create online instruction informed by neuroscience research and foundational educational psychology theories; and (5) continue to engage in the iterative process of online instruction improvement. These principles will look different online than they do in an in-person class, but they will produce the same student outcomes.

In order to implement the *Teachin' It!* model in an online or hybrid course, instructors need to have a deep understanding of the research and strategies in this book. For example, how will you include collaborative work and inquiry-based projects? How will you scaffold instruction and maximize the number of students learning in their reach zones? How will you minimize cognitive load and maximize germane load? What about tapping into prior knowledge? How can you ensure that you are creating a safe community of learners online? How can you foster a growth mindset experience where students take risks and learn from their mistakes? How will you alleviate stereotype threat?

Online learning introduces novel challenges in terms of asset-based instruction. Still there are some key elements and principles that apply. An instructor can still develop norms together with students about collaborating online and explicitly teach the protocol for how to use a forum and participate in online groups. An instructor can meet with groups of three or four students via Skype to discuss their group projects. Students can watch a Jo Boaler or Carol Dweck video on growth mindset. In an online course, it is easier to include videos of faculty of color and representation of students from more diverse backgrounds, and have guest speakers online who talk about college resources. Also, instructors can vet online texts and homework programs that are universally accessible for students. For example, XYZ Homework is affordable, has students of color represented on videos, provides videos in Spanish, offers growth mindset features like homework with no-penalties-for-multiple-attempts options, and is responsive to instructor suggestions.

THE POWER OF A COMMUNITY OF PRACTITIONERS

I prefer the term *community of practitioners*, rather than *community of practice*, because it is more person-centered. However, both expressions describe instructors working collaboratively to engage in the iterative cycle of instruction improvement. I interviewed more than 20 instructors for this book. Three instructor-researchers wrote chapters. Over 600 years of combined teaching expertise is contained on the pages of this book. This is what instructors can accomplish collaboratively that we cannot do individually—cache our resources (Figure 10.1).

Figure 10.1. Engaging in Communities of Practitioners

Instructors work in silos. Frequently, we develop our instructional approaches in isolation. We do not have ample opportunities to observe other instructors nor do we have extended collaboration time. While I listened to each instructor that I interviewed, I heard them describe different aspects of asset-based instruction. Each emphasized different strategies of the social constructivist model. It reminded me of the Buddhist story where six sages, in the dark, try to describe an elephant (Figure 10.2). The sage holding the tail says, "An elephant is swishy like a paintbrush." The sage touching the trunk says, "An elephant is flexible like a straw." The sages in this analogy are us—instructors, as we explore the potential of asset-based instruction. The elephant is the "It" with a capital "I" in *Teachin' It!* How can we explore and refine our approaches to instruction? By turning on the lights and talking to one another about our different perspectives and approaches.

We all have more expertise than we realize to offer a community of practitioners. What may seem like a simple strategy that you use every day can transform a colleague's instruction. For example, Regina Guerra told me, "Math is emotional." Dan Munton and Carlos Valencia offered strategies for memorizing names. Rafael Vasquez introduced the idea of calling students "colleagues." Laura Aspinall impressed on me the importance of using "people first" language. The implementation of these strat-

Figure 10.2. Six Sages Describe an Elephant in the Dark

egies transformed my instruction. Generally, we already have impromptu communities of practitioners, and we are already building a reservoir of shared knowledge.

Expertise is built on the shoulders of past researchers and educators, and it is co-constructed in communities of practitioners. Therefore, it is important that instructors are afforded opportunities to engage with other instructors to formally collaborate on how to improve outcomes for all students. Unfortunately, educators teach in silos and are seldom granted the luxury of paid time to collaborate with colleagues. Forming a community of practitioners at your college around a specific topic to continue to refine your instruction is a great way to build upon your shared expertise. Instructors can do peer observations, conduct **lesson plan studies,** form reading groups, or develop teams to tackle specific learning challenges. Other ways that you can connect with a wider group of educators are to: (1) join the *Teachin' It!* Facebook group or create your own; (2) build a reservoir of instructor videos or podcasts at your campus, as I did on the *Teachin' It!* YouTube Channel and Soundcloud Podcast; (3) attend and present at conferences; or (4) consult with an equity consultant like Dr. Derisa Grant at djmgconsulting.com to lead a campus community of practice on equity.

Teachin' It! is about disrupting systemic inequity, one classroom at a time. It provides ideas for illuminating and leveraging the assets of students who otherwise might not have access to 4-year degrees, including first-generation college students, students of color, non-native English speakers, and students with disabilities. Its goal is to help instructors deliver asset-based instruction that equalizes the playing field so that all students in our classes can actualize their full learning potential. For additional resources, visit www.feliciadarling.com.

References

Academic Senate for California Community Colleges (2006). *ESL Students in California Public Education*, Resolution number 15.02. Retrieved from www.asccc.org/resolutions/esl-students-california-public-higher-education

Addyman, C., & Mareschal, D. (2013). Local redundancy governs infants' spontaneous orienting to visual-temporal sequences. *Child Development, 84*(4), 1137–1144.

Alexander, M. (2012). *The new Jim Crow: Mass incarceration in the age of colorblindness.* New York, NY: New Press.

Allensworth, E., Nomi, T., Montgomery, N., & Lee, V. E. (2009). College preparatory curriculum for all: Consequences of ninth-grade course taking on academic outcomes in Chicago. *Educational Evaluation and Policy Analysis, 31*(4), 367–391.

American Association of Community Colleges. *Data points, 2018.* Retrieved from www.aacc.nche.edu/research-trends/datapoints/

An, B. P. (2013). The influence of dual enrollment on academic performance and college readiness: Differences by socioeconomic status. *Research in Higher Education, 54,* 407–432.

Anderson, L. W., & Krathwohl, D. R. (2001). *A taxonomy for learning, teaching, and assessing: A revision of Bloom's taxonomy of educational objectives* (abridged ed.). Boston, MA: Allyn & Bacon.

Anderson, R. K., Boaler, J., & Dieckmann, J. A. (2018). Achieving elusive teacher change through challenging myths about learning: A blended approach. *Education Sciences, 8*(3), 98.

Aronson, J., Fried, C., & Good, C. (2002). Reducing the effects of stereotype threat on African American college students by shaping theories of intelligence. *Journal of Experimental Social Psychology, 38,* 113–125.

Attinasi, J. J. (1997). Racism, language variety, and urban minorities: Issues in bilingualism and bidialectalism. In A. Darder, R. D. Torres, & H. Gutiérrez (Eds.), *Latinos and education: A critical reader* (pp. 279–301). New York, NY: Routledge.

Bailey, T., Belfield, C., & Benson, J. (2015). Is college worth it, and for whom? Retrieved from capseecenter.org/is-college-worth-it-and-for-whom/

Bereiter, C., & Engelmann, S. (1966). *Teaching disadvantaged children in the preschool.* Englewood Cliffs, NJ: Prentice-Hall.

Berk, L., & Winsler, A. (1995). Vygotsky: His life and works and Vygotsky's approach to development. In *Scaffolding children's learning: Vygotsky and early childhood learning* (pp. 25–34). Washington, DC: National Association for the Education of Young Children.

Berteletti, I., & Booth, J. R. (2015). Perceiving fingers in single-digit arithmetic problems. *Frontiers in Psychology, 6,* 226. Retrieved from doi.org/10.3389/fpsyg.2015.00226

Blackwell, L. S., Trzesniewski, K. H., & Dweck, C. S. (2007). Implicit theories of intelligence predict achievement across an adolescent transition: A longitudinal study and an intervention. *Child Development, 78,* 246–263.

Bloom, B. S. (1969). *Taxonomy of educational objectives: The classification of educational goals: Handbook 1. Cognitive domain.* Montréal, Canada: Education Nouvelle.

Blum, S. D. (2016). *"I love learning: I hate school": An anthropology of college.* Ithaca, NY: Cornell University Press.

Boaler, J. (2002). *Experiencing school mathematics: Traditional and reform approaches to teaching and their impact on student learning* (Rev. ed.). New York, NY: Routledge.

Boaler, J. (2016). *Mathematical mindsets: Unleashing students' potential through creative math, inspiring messages and innovative teaching.* San Francisco, CA: Jossey-Bass.

Borko, H., & Whitcomb, J. (2008). Teachers, teaching, and teacher education: Comments on the National Mathematics Advisory Panel's report. *Educational Researcher, 34*(9), 565–572.

Canning, E. C., Muenks, K., Green, D. J., & Murphy, M. C. (2019). STEM faculty who believe ability is fixed have larger racial achievement gaps and inspire less student motivation in their classes. *Science Advances, 5*(2), 1–7.

Carnoy, M., Jacobsen, R., Mishel, L., & Rothstein, R. (2005). *The charter school dust-up: Examining the evidence on enrollment and achievement.* Washington, DC: Economic Policy Institute.

Center for Research on Education Outcomes (CREDO). (2009). *Multiple choice: Charter school performance in 16 states.* Stanford University Stanford, CA. Retrieved from credo.stanford.edu/reports/MULTIPLE_CHOICE_CREDO.pdf

Center for Research on Education Outcomes. (2015). *Urban charter school study: Report on 41 regions.* Stanford University Stanford, CA. Retrieved from urbancharters.stanford.edu/summary.php

Cohen, E. G., Lotan, R. A. (2004). Equity in heterogeneous classrooms. In J.A. Banks and C.A.M. Banks (Eds.), *Handbook of research on multicultural education* (pp. 736–750). San Francisco, CA: Jossey-Bass.

Cohen, E. G., Lotan, R., Scarloss, B., & Arellano, A. R. (1999). Complex instruction: Equity in cooperative learning classrooms. *Theory Into Practice, 38*(2), 80–86.

Cohen, G., Garcia, J., Apfel, N., & Master, A. (2006). Reducing the racial achievement gap: A social-psychological intervention. *Science, 313*(5791), 1307–1310.

Cohen, G. L., Steele, C. M., & Ross, L. D. (1999). The mentor's dilemma: Providing critical feedback across the racial divide. *Personality and Social Psychology Bulletin, 25*(10), 1302–1318.

Connell, C. (2008). The vital role of community colleges in the education and integration of immigrants. Retrieved from www.cccie.org/reports/ vital-role-community-colleges-education-integration-immigrants/

Cook, V. (2008). *Second language learning and language teaching.* London, England: Hodder Education.

Cooper, J. N., & Hawkins, B. (2016). An anti-deficit perspective on black male student athletes' educational experiences at a historically black college/university. *Race, Ethnicity and Education, 19*(5), 950–979.

Corwin, Z. B., & Tierney, W. G. (2007). *Getting there—and beyond: Building a culture of college-going in high schools.* Report from USC Center for Higher Education Policy Analysis. Retrieved from files.eric.ed.gov/fulltext/ ED498731.pdf

Darder, A. (1997). Creating the conditions for cultural democracy in the classroom. In A. Darder, R. D. Torres, & H. Gutiérrez (Eds.), *Latinos and education: A critical reader* (pp. 331–350). New York, NY: Routledge.

Darling, F. (2017). Outsider indigenous research: Dancing the tightrope between etic and emic perspectives. *Forum: Qualitative Social Research, 17*(3), 1–7.

Darling, F. (in press). Incorporating cultural assets in Yucatec Maya math classrooms: Opportunities missed? *Journal of Mathematics and Culture.*

Darling-Hammond, L. (2004). Standards, accountability, and school reform. *Teachers College Record, 106*(6), 1047–1085.

Darling-Hammond, L., & Prince, C. D. (2007). *Strengthening teacher quality in high-need schools: Policy and practice.* Washington, DC: Council of Chief State School Officers.

Darling-Hammond, L., & Youngs, P. (2002). Defining "highly qualified teachers": What does "scientifically-based research" actually tell us? *Educational Researcher, 31*(9), 13–25.

Diamond, J. B. (2008). Cultivating a school-based discourse that emphasizes teachers' responsibility for student learning. In M. Pollock (Ed.), *Everyday antiracism: Concrete ways to successfully navigate the relevance of race in school.* New York, NY: New Press.

DuBois, W. E. B. (1903). *The Souls of Black folk.* Chicago, IL: A. C. McClurg.

Duckworth, A. (2016). *Grit: The power of passion and perseverance.* New York, NY: Scribner.

Dweck, C. S. (2006). *Mindset: The new psychology of success.* New York, NY: Random House.

Dweck, C. S. (2007). The perils and promises of praise. *Educational Leadership,* *65*(2), 34–39.

Farmer-Hinton, R. (2008). Social capital and college planning: Students of color using school networks for support and guidance. *Education and Urban Society, 41*(1), 127–157.

Farmer-Hinton, R. (2011). On being college prep: Examining the implementation of a "college for all" mission in an urban charter school. *Urban Review, 43*(5), 567–596.

Fields, R. D. (2010). Why can some blind people process speech faster than sighted persons? *Scientific American.* Retrieved from www.scientificamerican. com/article/why-can-some-blind-people-process/

Frankenberg, E., Siegel-Hawley, G., & Wang, J. (2011). Choice without equity: Charter school segregation. *Educational Policy Analysis Archives, 19*(1). doi: dx.doi.org/10.14507/epaa.v19n1.2011

Freire, P. (2000). *Pedagogy of the oppressed.* New York, NY: Continuum.

Gándara P., & Contreras, F. (2009). *The Latino education crisis: The consequences of failed social policies.* Cambridge, MA: Harvard University Press.

Geronimus, A. T., Pearson, J. A., Linnenbringer, E., Schulz, A. J., Reyes, A. G., Epel, E. S., . . . Blackburn, E. H. (2015). Race-ethnicity, poverty, urban stressors, and telomere length in a Detroit community-based sample. *Journal of Health and Social Behavior, 56*(2), 199–224.

Gibbon, J. (2015) Meeting the Extraordinary Cameron [blog post]. Retrieved on March 1, 2019 from http://www.pbs.org/the-brain-with-david-eagleman/blogs/behind-the-scenes-blog/meeting-the-extraordinary-cameron/

Golann, J. W. (2015). The paradox of success at a no-excuses school. *Sociology of Education, 88*(2), 103–119.

Goldrick-Rab, S., Richardson, J., Schneider, J., Hernandez, A., & Cady, C. (2018). *Still hungry and homeless in college.* University of Wisconsin, Wisconsin Hope Lab, Madison, Wisconsin.

Gonzalez, N., Moll, L., & Amanti, C. (Eds.). (2005). *Funds of knowledge: Theorizing practices in households, communities, and classrooms.* Mahwah, NJ: Routledge.

Good, C., Aronson, J., & Inzlicht, M. (2003). Improving adolescents' standardized test performance: An intervention to reduce the effects of stereotype threat. *Journal of Applied Developmental Psychology, 24*(6), 645–662.

Goodman, S., & Fine, M. (2018). *It's not about grit: Trauma, inequity, and the power of transformative teaching.* New York, NY: Teachers College Press.

Harper, S. R. (2009). Institutional seriousness concerning black male student engagement: Necessary conditions and collaborative partnerships. In S. R. Harper & S. J. Quaye (Eds.), *Student engagement in higher education: Theoretical perspectives and practical approaches for diverse populations* (pp. 137–156). New York, NY: Routledge.

Harper, S. R. (2010). An anti-deficit achievement framework for research on students of color in STEM. *New Directions for Institutional Research, 2010*(148), 63–74.

Hess, R. D., & Shipman, V. C. (1965). Early experience and the socialization of cognitive modes in children. *Child Development, 36*(4), 869–886.

Hill, L. D. (2008). School strategies and the "college-linking" process: Reconsidering the effects of high schools on college enrollment. *Sociology of Education, 81*(1), 53–76.

Holland, N. E., & Farmer-Hinton, R. (2009). Leave no schools behind: The importance of a college culture in urban public high schools. *The High School Journal, 92*(3), 24–43.

Hotchkins, B. K. (2016). African American males navigate racial microaggressions. *Teachers College Record, 118*(6), 1–36.

Hubbard, L., & Kulkarni, R. (2009). Charter schools: Learning from the past, planning for the future. *Journal of Education Change, 10*(2–3), 173–189.

Hubbell, L., & Hubbell, K. (2010). When a college class becomes a mob: Coping with student cohorts. *College Student Journal, 44*(2), 340–353.

Huston, T. (2006). Race and gender bias in higher education: Could faculty course evaluations impede further progress toward parity? *Seattle Journal for Social Justice, 4*(2), Article 34.

Johnson-Ahorlu, R. (2013). "Our biggest challenge is stereotypes": Understanding stereotype threat and the academic experiences of African American undergraduates. *Journal of Negro Education, 82*(4), 382–392.

Keigher, A. (2010). *Teacher attrition and mobility: Results from the 2008–09 teacher follow-up survey* (NCES 2010-353). Washington, DC: U.S. Department of Education, National Center for Education Statistics.

KIPP Foundation. (2012). The KIPP 2011 annual report card. Retrieved from www.kipp.org/results/annual-report-card/2011-report-card

Krashen, S. T. (1982). *Principles and practice in second language acquisition*. Oxford, England: Pergamon.

Krendl, A. C., Richeson, J. A., Kelley, W. M., & Heatherton, T. F. (2008). The negative consequences of threat: A functional magnetic resonance imaging investigation of the neural mechanisms underlying women's underperformance in math. *Psychological Science. 19*(2), 168–175.

Krogstad, J. M. (2016). 5 facts about Latinos and education. PEW Research Center. Retrieved from www.pewresearch.org/fact-tank/2016/07/28/5-facts-about-latinos-and-education/

Lareau, A. (2003). *Unequal childhoods: Class, race, and family life*. Oakland, CA: University of California Press.

Lave, J., & Wenger, E. (1991). *Situated learning: Legitimate peripheral participation*. New York, NY: Cambridge University Press.

Lee, D. B., Kim, E. S., & Neblett, E. W., Jr. (2017). The link between discrimination and telomere length in African American adults. *Health Psychology, 36*(5), 458–467.

Lee, J. M., & Ransom, T. (2011). *The educational experience of young men of color.* New York, NY: College Board.

Lucas, T., Henze, R., and Donato, R. (1990). Promoting the success of Latino language-minority students: An exploratory study of six high schools. *Harvard Educational Review,* 60(3), 315–341.

MacDonald, V. M. & Carrillo, J. F. (2006). Review of the book *Chicanas andChicanos in School: Racial Profiling, Identity Battles, and Empowerment,* by M. Pizarro. *International Journal of Qualitative Studies in Education, 19,* 1.

MacNell, L., Driscoll, A., & Hunt, A. N. (2015). What's in a name? Exposing gender bias in student ratings of teaching. *Innovative Higher Education,* 40(4), 291–303.

Marian, V., Shildkrot, Y., Blumenfeld, H. K., Kaushanskaya, M., Faroqi-Shah, Y., & Hirsch, J. (2007). Cortical activation during word processing in late bilinguals: Similarities and differences as revealed by functional magnetic resonance imaging. *Journal of Clinical and Experimental Neuropsychology,* 29(3), 247–265.

Marzano, R. J. (2007). *The art and science of teaching.* Alexandria, VA: Association for Supervision and Curriculum Development.

Mathur, B., Epel, E., Kind, S., Desai, M., Parks, C. G., Sandler, P., & Khazeni, N. (2016). Perceived stress and telomere length: A systematic review, meta-analysis, and methodologic considerations for advancing the field. *Brain, Behavior, and Immunity, 54*(5), 158–169.

McCandliss, B. D., Beck, I. L., Sandak, R., & Perfetti, C. A. (2003). Focusing attention on decoding for children with poor reading skills: Design and preliminary tests of the word building intervention. *Scientific Studies of Reading, 7*(1), 75–104.

McDermott, R. (1993). The acquisition of a child by a learning disability. In S. Chaiklin & J. Lave (Eds.), *Understanding practice: Perspectives on activity and context.* Cambridge, England: Cambridge University Press.

McKown, C., & Weinstein, R. (2008). Teacher expectations, classroom context, and the achievement gap. *Journal of School Psychology, 6*(3), 235–261.

Mead, K. (2016). Interview: Dolores Huerta discusses grassroots activism and weaving movements. The San Diego Foundation. Retrieved from www.sdfoundation.org/news-events/sdf-news/interview-dolores-huerta-discusses-grassroots-activism-and-weaving-movements/

Meade, E. E. (2014). Overview of community characteristics in areas with concentrated poverty. U.S. Department of Health & Human Services, Office of the Assistant Secretary for Planning and Evaluation. Retrieved from aspe.hhs.gov/report/overview-community-characteristics-areas-concentrated-poverty

Medina, J. (2014). *Brain rules: 12 principles for surviving and thriving at work, home, and school.* Seattle, WA: Pear Press.

Mejia, M. C., Rodriguez, O., & Johnson, H. (2016). *Preparing students for success in California's community colleges.* Public Policy Institute of California. Retrieved from www.ppic.org/content/pubs/report/R_1116MMR. pdf

Menon, V. (2014). Arithmetic in the child and adult brain. In *The Oxford handbook of numerical cognition.* doi: 10.1093/oxfordhb/9780199642342.013.041

Miller, G. E., Yu, T., Chen, E., & Brody, G. H. (2015). Self-control forecasts better psychosocial outcomes but faster epigenetic aging in low-SES youth. *Proceedings of the National Academy of Sciences, 112*(33), 10325–10330.

Moll, L. C., Amanti, C., Neff, D., Gonzalez, N. (1992). Funds of knowledge for teaching: Using a qualitative approach to connect homes and classrooms. *Theory into Practice, 31*(2), 132–141.

Moser, J. S., Schroder, H. S., Heeter, C., Moran, T. P., & Lee, Y. H. (2011). Mind your errors: Evidence for a neural mechanism linking growth mindset to adaptive posterior adjustments. *Psychological Science, 22*(12), 1484–1489.

Mueller, J. C. (2017). Producing colorblindness: Everyday mechanisms of white ignorance. *Social Problems, 64*(2), 219–238.

Mueller, C. M., & Dweck, C. S. (1998). Praise for intelligence can undermine children's motivation and performance. *Journal of Personal and Social Psychology, 75*(1), 33–52.

Musu-Gillette, L., Robinson, J., McFarland, J., KewalRamani, A., Zhang, A., & Wilkinson-Flicker, S. (2016). *Status and trends in the education of racial and ethnic groups 2016* (NCES 2016-007). Washington, DC: U.S. Department of Education, National Center for Education Statistics.

National Alliance for Public Charter Schools. (2012). Details from the dashboard: Charter school race/ethnicity demographics. Retrieved from www. publiccharters.org/sites/default/files/migrated/wp-content/uploads/ 2014/01/NAPCS-2010-2011-Race_Ethnicity-Details-from-the-Dashboard_20120516T152831.pdf

National Center for Education Statistics. (2018a). Educational attainment of young adults. The condition of education. Retrieved from nces.ed.gov/programs/coe/pdf/coe_caa.pdf

National Center for Education Statistics. (2018b). Public charter school enrollment. The condition of education. Retrieved from nces.ed.gov/ pubs2018/2018144.pdf

Newman, L., Wagner, M., Cameto, R., & Knokey, A. M. (2009). *The post-high school outcomes of youth with disabilities up to 4 years after high school. A report of findings from the National Longitudinal Transition Study-2 (NLTS2).* Menlo Park, CA: SRI International.

Okamoto, S. K. (2010). Academic Marginalization? The Journalistic Response to Social Work Research on Native Hawaiian Youths. *Social Work, 55*(1), 93–94.

Olsen, R. K., Pangelinan, M. M., Bogulski, C., Chakravarty, M. M., Luk, G.,

Grady, C., & Bialystok, E. (2015). The effect of lifelong bilingualism on regional grey and white matter volume. *Brain Research, 1612,* 128–139.

Osborne, J. W. (2007). Linking stereotype threat and anxiety. *Educational Psychology, 27*(1), 135–154.

Osler, J. (2007). *A guide for integrating issues of social and economic justice into mathematics curriculum.* Retrieved from www.radicalmath.org/docs/SJMathGuide.pdf

Parker, W. M., Puig, A., Johnson, J., & Anthony, C., Jr. (2016). Black males on white campuses: Still invisible men? *College Student Affairs Journal, 34*(3), 76–92.

Paul, R., Elder, L., & Foundation for Critical Thinking. (2016). The thinker's guide to the art of Socratic questioning: Based on critical thinking concepts & tools. Retrieved from www.criticalthinking.org/store/get_file.php?inventories_id=231&inventories_files_id=374

Perry, A. (2016). Black and brown boys don't need to learn grit; they need schools to stop being racist. *The Root.* Retrieved from www.theroot.com/black-and-brown-boys-don-t-need-to-learn-grit-they-nee-1790855155

Piaget, J. (1952). *The origins of intelligence in children* (M. Cook, Trans.). New York, NY: Norton.

Powers, J. T., Cook, J. E., Purdie-Vaughns, V., Garcia, J., Apfel, N., & Cohen, G., L. (2016). Changing environments by changing individuals: The emergent effects of psychological intervention. *Psychological Sciences, 27*(2), 150–160.

Price, G. R., Mazzocco, M. M., & Ansari, D. (2013). Why mental arithmetic counts: Brain activation during single digit arithmetic predicts high school math scores. *The Journal of Neuroscience, 33*(1), 156–163.

Rattan, A., Good, C., & Dweck, C. S. (2012). "It's ok —Not everyone can be good at math": Instructors with an entity theory comfort (and demotivate) students. *Journal of Experimental Social Psychology, 48*(3), 731–737.

Redford, J., & Mulvaney Hoyer, K. (2017). *First-generation and continuing-generation college students: A comparison of high school and postsecondary experiences.* National Center for Education Statistics. Retrieved from nces.ed.gov/pubs2018/2018009.pdf

Rhodes, C. (2017). *Boosting Chinese ESL students' active participation in classrooms in the U.S.: A handbook for teachers* (Unpublished thesis). University of San Francisco, San Francisco, CA.

Rogoff, B., & Morelli, G. (1989). Perspectives on children's development from cultural psychology. *American Psychologist, 44*(2), 343–348.

Rogoff, B., Paradise, R., Arauz, R. M., Correa-Chávez, M., & Angelillo, C. (2003). Firsthand learning through intent participation. *Annual Review of Psychology, 54*(1), 175–203.

Romeo, K. (2000). Krashen and Terrell's "natural approach." Retrieved from web.stanford.edu/~hakuta/www/LAU/ICLangLit/NaturalApproach.htm

Rumbaut, R. G., & Ima, K. (1988). The adaptation of southeast Asian refugee youth: A comparative study. San Diego, CA: San Diego State University. Retrieved from eric.ed.gov/?id=ED299372

Sapon-Shevin, M. (2004). Introduction. In E. G. Cohen, C. M. Brody, & M. Sapon-Shevin (Eds.), *Teaching cooperative learning: The challenge for teacher education* (pp. 1–12). Albany, NY: SUNY Press.

Senninger, T. (2000). *Abenteuer Leiten in Abenteuern lernen: Methodenset zur Planung und Leitung kooperativer Lerngemeinschaften für Training und Teamentwicklung in Schule.* [Adventure Learning in adventure: Lessons for planning and leading cooperative learning communities for training and team development in school.] Münster, Germany: Öktopia Verlag.

Shapiro, D., Dundar, A., Huie, F., Wakhungu, P., Yuan, X., Nathan, A., & Hwang, Y. A. (2017). *Completing college: A national view of student attainment rates by race and ethnicity—fall 2010 cohort* (Signature Report No. 12b). Herndon, VA: National Student Clearinghouse Research Center.

Smith, Q. P. (2017). *An anti-deficit approach to understanding bachelor's degree attainment among African Americans at a predominantly white institution.* ProQuest. Retrieved from eric.ed.gov/?id=ED578639

Smith, W. A., Hung, M., & Franklin, J. D. (2011). Racial battle fatigue and the "mis"education of black men: Racial microaggressions, societal problems, and environmental stress. *Journal of Negro Education, 80*(1), 63–82.

Smith, W. A., Mustaffa, J. B., Jones, C. M., Curry, T. J., & Allen, W. R. (2016). 'You make me wanna holler and throw up both my hands!': Campus culture, Black misandric microaggressions, and racial battle fatigue. *International Journal of Qualitative Studies in Education, 29*(9), 1189–1209.

Smith, W. A., Yosso, T. J., & Solórzano, D. G. (2007). Racial primes and black misandry on historically white campuses: Toward critical race accountability in educational administration. *Educational Administration Quarterly, 43*(5), 559–585.

Spohn, C. C. (2000). Thirty years of sentencing reform: The quest for a racially neutral sentencing process. *Criminal Justice, 3*, 427–502.

Steele, C. (2010). *Whistling Vivaldi: And other clues to how stereotypes affect us.* New York, NY: Norton.

Steele, C. M., & Aronson, J. (1995). Stereotype threat and the intellectual test performance of African Americans. *Journal of Personality and Social Psychology, 69*, 797–811.

Stenning, K., Schmoelz, A., Wren, H., Stouraitis, E., Scaltsas, T., Alexopoulos, C., & Aichhorn, A. (2016). Socratic dialogue as a teaching and research method for co-creativity? *Digital Culture & Education, 8*(2), 154–168.

Suárez-Orozco, C., Suárez-Orozco, M. M., & Todorova, I. (2010). *Learning a new land: Immigrant students in American society.* Cambridge, MA: Harvard University Press.

Sweller, J., Ayres, P., & Kalyuga, S. (2011). *Cognitive load theory*. New York, NY: Springer.

U.S. Department of Justice. (2015, March 4). Investigation of the Ferguson Police Department. Retrieved from www.justice.gov/sites/default/files/opa/press-releases/attachments/2015/03/04/ferguson_police_department_report.pdf

Uttl, B., White, C. A., & Wong Gonzalez, D. (2017). Meta-analysis of faculty's teaching effectiveness: Student evaluation of teaching ratings and student learning are not related. *Studies in Educational Evaluation, 54*, 22–42.

Valdés, G. (2001). *Learning and not learning English: Latino students in American schools*. New York, NY: Teachers College Press.

Van den Bergh, L., Denessen, E., Hornstra, L., Voeten, M., & Holland, R. W. (2010). The implicit prejudiced attitudes of teachers: Relations to teacher expectations and the ethnic achievement gap. *American Educational Research Journal, 47*(2), 497–527.

Vygotsky, L. S. (1978). *Mind in society: The development of higher psychological processes*. Cambridge, MA: Harvard University Press.

Walker, J. D., Cotner, S., Baepler, P., & Decker, M. (2008). A delicate balance: Integrating active learning into a large lecture course. *CBE Life Sciences Education, 7*(4), 361–367.

Walton, G. M., & Cohen, G. L. (2007). A question of belonging: Race, social fit, and achievement. *Journal of Personality and Social Psychology, 92*(1), 82–96.

Walton, G. M., & Cohen, G. L. (2011). A brief social-belonging intervention improves academic and health outcomes of minority students. *Science, 331,* 1447–1451.

Washington, M. (2013). Is the black male college graduate becoming an endangered species? A multi-case analysis of the attrition of black males in higher education. *LUX: A Journal of Transdisciplinary Writing and Research from Claremont Graduate University, 3*(1).

Watts, J. (2013). Why hyper-bonding occurs in the learning community classroom and what to do about it. *Learning Communities Research and Practice, 1*(3).

Wenger, E., McDermott, R., & Snyder, W. (2002). *Cultivating communities of practice: A guide to managing knowledge*. Cambridge, MA: Harvard Business School Press.

Werwath, T. S. (2016). *Academic marginalization in high school as a predictor of depressive symptoms in midlife* (Master's thesis). University of Texas at Austin. Retrieved from repositories.lib.utexas.edu/handle/2152/41979

Yeager, D. S., Purdie-Vaughns, V., Garcia, J., Apfel, N., Brzustoski, P., Master, A., . . . Williams, M. E. (2014). Breaking the cycle of mistrust: Wise interventions to provide critical feedback across the racial divide. *Journal of Experimental Psychology: General, 143,* 804–824.

Yerkes R. M. & Dodson, J.D. (1908). The relation of strength of stimulus to rapidity of habit-formation. *Journal of Comparative Neurology and Psychology*, *18*(5), 459–482.

Yoncheva, Y., Wise, J., & McCandliss, B. D. (2015). Hemispheric specialization for visual words is shaped by attention to sublexical units during initial learning. *Brain and Language*, *145*, 23–33.

Zimmer, R., Gill, B., Booker, K., Lavertu, S., & Witte, J. (2012). Examining charter student achievement effects across seven states. *Economics of Education Review*, *31*(2), 213–224.

Zinn, H. (2015). *A people's history of the United States*. New York, NY: Harper.

Index

About the Author

Felicia Darling is a first-generation college student who has taught math and education courses for 30 years at both the secondary and college levels. She possesses a PhD in Math Education from Stanford University and is a Fulbright Scholar for her research in Yucatec Maya classrooms. Her work focuses on students who are underrepresented among those with 4-year degrees—especially students of color, students with disabilities, and first-generation college, LGBTQ+, and bilingual students. Her *Teachin' It!* instructional model illuminates the assets of students in the classroom. Currently, Felicia is a mathematics instructor in the College Skills Department at Santa Rosa Junior College.

About Contributed Chapter Authors

Luz Navarette García has an EdD in International and Multicultural Education and Second Language Acquisition from the University of San Francisco. She is a full-time instructor in the English as a Second Language Department at Santa Rosa Junior College.

Christine Victoria Rodriguez has a PhD in Developmental and Psychological Sciences in Education from Stanford University. She is an education psychology professor, scholar, and researcher who specializes in college readiness for first-generation Latinx college students.

Michael L. Washington has a PhD in in Postsecondary Education from Claremont Graduate University. He is a professor, educational sociologist, and qualitative researcher.